The T(
Guide for 1
Manageme   ⎯⎯ᴜᵤ EdItion

"Immensely useful for teachers . . . Knoster knows how to communicate his practical messages so that teachers and students will benefit." —**Glen Dunlap, Ph.D.**, University of Nevada, Reno, and University of South Florida

"Filled with practical strategies . . . The advice offered in any single standalone chapter is likely to make a substantial improvement in any teacher's classroom. Teachers can step in at any chapter depending on their need, and even seasoned teachers can pick up new and state-of-the-art strategies to improve the classroom environment." —**Lee Kern, Ph.D.,** Lehigh University

"Clear, useful strategies to help teachers effectively prevent and respond to challenging behaviors . . . Knoster provides teachers with a helpful context to decode difficult behavior and then follows with detailed, practical strategies that teachers can easily apply in their own classrooms." —**Bridget Walker, Ph.D.,** Seattle University

"You want classroom-friendly tips, practical examples, and ready-to-use guidelines—then [this book] is the perfect resource. Even better, they are evidence-based and applicable at all grade levels." —**George Sugai, Ph.D.,** Neag School of Education, University of Connecticut

"Tim Knoster offers a practical approach to effective classroom management, focusing on research-based prevention and early intervention strategies. He has put all the pieces together for educators to create a healthy and positive learning environment." —**Lori Newcomer, Ph.D.,** University of Missouri

The Teacher's Pocket Guide for Effective Classroom Management

The Teacher's Pocket Guide for Effective Classroom Management

Second Edition

by

Tim Knoster, Ed.D.

Bloomsburg University of Pennsylvania

· P A U L · H ·
BROOKES
PUBLISHING Cº ®

Baltimore • London • Sydney

Paul H. Brookes Publishing Co.
Post Office Box 10624
Baltimore, MD 21285-0624

www.brookespublishing.com

Typeset by Scribe Inc., Philadelphia, Pennsylvania.
Manufactured in the United States of America by
Versa Press, Inc., East Peoria, Illinois.

Cover image © istockphoto.com/vgajic. Clip art © 2014 Jupiterimages Corporation.

Individuals described in this book are composites or real people whose situations are
masked and are based on the author's experiences. In all instances, names and identifying details have been changed to protect confidentiality.

Library of Congress Cataloging-in-Publication Data
Knoster, Tim, 1956–
    The teacher's pocket guide for effective classroom management / by Tim Knoster,
Ed.D.—Second edition.
        pages   cm
    Includes bibliographical references.
    ISBN 978-1-59857-402-9 (pbk. : alk. paper)—ISBN 1-59857-402-7 (pbk. : alk. paper)—
ISBN 978-1-59857-498-2 (epub e-book)—ISBN 1-59857-498-1 (epub e-book)
    1. Classroom management. 2. Effective teaching.   I. Title.

    LB3013.K63 2014
    371.102'4—dc23   2013029618

British Library Cataloguing in Publication data are available from the British Library.

2018   2017   2016   2015   2014

10   9   8   7   6   5   4   3   2   1

Contents

Contents

About the Reproducible Materials

Purchasers of this book may download, print, and/or photocopy the Expectations Planning Matrix, Behavior Progress Report (Primary Classroom), Behavior Progress Report (Middle or Secondary Classroom), and Monitoring Achievement of 4:1 Ratio for educational use. These materials are included with the print book and are also available at **www.brookespublishing.com/knoster/eforms** for both print and e-book buyers.

So Who Is This Guy?

Tim Knoster, Ed.D., is Professor and Chair-
person of the Department of Exceptional-
ity Programs in the College of Education
at Bloomsburg University of Pennsylvania.
Dr. Knoster, in collaboration with colleagues,
established the McDowell Institute for
Teacher Excellence in Positive Behavior Support at Bloomsburg University in 2012, which
emphasizes the translation of research on
positive behavior intervention and support into practical
application for practice by teachers in schools. In addition,
Dr. Knoster has served as Executive Director of the inter-
national Association for Positive Behavior Support (APBS)
since its inception in 2003. Dr. Knoster (or Tim, as he prefers) has been involved with preservice and in-service
teacher training since the mid-1980s. He has worn many
hats throughout his career, including that of classroom
teacher, director of student support services and special
education, and principal investigator on federal projects
focused on classroom and student-centered behavior intervention and support. Specifically relevant to this book,
Dr. Knoster has extensive experience in providing professional development for classroom teachers throughout the
United States and Canada and has been the recipient of
various awards for his endeavors in this regard. He has
extensively published manuscripts, training materials,
and other practitioner-oriented resources concerning the
linkages among research, policy, and practice in the classroom. Dr. Knoster has an uncanny ability to help teachers
interpret the research literature on behavioral matters in

a way that enables them to translate that same research into practical strategies and approaches in their classrooms. Along these same lines, Dr. Knoster has a national reputation of being a dynamic advocate, leader, and presenter concerning classroom management and student-centered behavior intervention and support.

Acknowledgments

Given that we are all influenced by so many people in our lives, it would require a better memory than I have, coupled with too many pages for the publisher, to list specific names of all the professional colleagues and mentors who have influenced my work over the years. So, rather than try to create an exhaustive who's-who list (as well as run the risk of inadvertently leaving someone of great importance out), I would like to acknowledge a few groups (or networks) of people in this regard.

First, I would like to thank my friends and colleagues involved with both the Association for Positive Behavior Support and the Positive Behavior Approaches Committee of TASH for the influence that they have had on my orientation to addressing behavioral concerns. My friends and colleagues within these networks know who they are and also operate from a similar perspective as mine in sharing the understanding that it is our collective work (rather than the work by any one of us as individuals) that really matters.

In addition, I would like to acknowledge the professional challenges, encouragement, and support that I have received from my friends within the advocacy community in tandem with the countless numbers of teachers (and prospective teachers) with whom I have had the privilege to interact and collaborate over the years. Furthermore, it is these same people who have helped keep me grounded in practical matters that mean the most to families and teachers and who continually remind me that although the work we do is important, I should not take myself too seriously.

Finally, and most important, I want to acknowledge as well as dedicate this book to my family and close friends who provide the color and flavor in my life. None of us is an island to himself or herself, and in this regard, it is these same people to whom I am indebted beyond my ability to repay—in particular to my wife Marsha and our three children (Megan, Kevin, and Kelsey). You continue to provide meaning to my life along with the inspiration and support to share my thoughts (for better or worse).

So Why Should I Read This Book?

I believe there are a number of good reasons why you should read this book, with the most important reason being that you should find the content helpful if you work directly (or aspire to work directly) with young children or adolescents in a classroom setting. Let's face it—anyone who works with kids in schools knows first-hand the rewards and challenges (the proverbial roller-coaster ride of emotions with the highs and lows) that we can experience in our classrooms daily. Teachers have personal understanding of these shared experiences, whether it be big hugs or big tears from a kindergartener, high-fives for a job well done or sneers over assigned work from a middle-schooler, or a smile for your effort in providing support or a look of "what are looking at" from a junior who earned a poor grade on a project or test. If truth in advertising were provided to aspiring teachers, the statement "Teaching can be simultaneously exhilarating and hazardous to your health and is not recommended for the faint of heart." would be visibly posted on the walls at all teacher preparatory institutions. The professional expectation to effectively teach all students becomes even more daunting with increasing demands for academic student performance, as primarily measured through high-stakes testing, along with (what at least feels like at times) the publicly posted bull's-eye or "kick me" sign that we as teachers collectively wear on our backs in the eyes of some factions within our society, as evidenced through various school reform initiatives in tandem with increased public scrutiny in teacher performance evaluations (not that the notion of utilizing more functional measures is not a laudable idea; rather, the idea can unfortunately be lost as a result of political agendas). Furthermore, the challenge of teaching is complex given the increasing array of needs presented by students in our classrooms, especially when you consider that prevalent research suggests that perhaps as many as one out of every five students in our schools today may have, at some point in time, exhibited some level of emotional or behavioral impairment. It is with a firsthand understanding of this societal context that I set out to write the second edition to this book, with the primary goal continuing to be to provide my fellow teachers with a helpful, user-friendly resource to guide the establishment of a healthy classroom environment for student learning. The bottom line is that teachers have historically been, and continue to be, the single most important external catalyst outside of the family for students achieving academic, social, and emotional learning outcomes. By this I do *not* mean that any teacher, regardless of how great he or she may be, can accomplish such outcomes alone. Rather, I simply mean that when we look at the many external factors and resources that are provided in schools today that influence student learning, the quality of any given student's teacher is the single most important factor. I believe you will find this book, which in reality is somewhat akin to a *SparkNotes* version, or connecting the dots of what I call "foundational classroom management procedures," valuable whether you are an aspiring middle or high school teacher or a veteran of more than 20 years in a primary classroom. You should find these procedures useful regardless of the age of your students as well as the presence of things outside of your control as a teacher, including issues of poverty, the presence or absence of family and community support, or identified student disabilities. Simply stated, I do not want to waste your time in reading (or my time in writing) the second edition of this book for its own sake. The initial edition of *The Teacher's Pocket Guide for Effective Classroom Management* highlighted effective classroom management procedures. Given this, why reinvent the wheel? This second edition is again written in a conversational tone as was the first edition, using first-person language, which I have used in workshops and in-service training with thousands of classroom teachers throughout my teaching career. The practices and approaches described in this second edition continue to be based in the literature on classroom management and therefore reflect evidence-based practice. However, various enhancements have been added to this second edition that both are consistent with the preventative orientation of the first edition and further frame the application of the practices described throughout this book within the context of what has come to be described as a multitiered systems of support (MTSS) framework in the form of schoolwide positive behavior intervention and support (SWPBIS). Although increasing numbers of schools are implementing positive behavior intervention and support (PBIS) with varying degrees of fidelity, there remains a large number of school systems, for whatever their reasons, that have not (as of yet) fully adopted this approach in their local schools. In light of this reality, I have provided guidance in this second edition for teachers who find themselves working within schools that have formally adopted and are utilizing a PBIS approach as well as for educators who are teaching within more traditional school settings. I have also provided a list of recommended

> Teaching can be simultaneously exhilarating and hazardous to your health and is not recommended for the faint of heart.

resources for you in the References and Resources for Further Reading of this second edition should you desire to have access to the expansive base of literature that supports the practices that I have incorporated into these chapters. I am optimistic that you will find this book, as was the case with the first edition, to be an easy read in terms of concepts and practices. Although each chapter can stand alone, I encourage you to look at the approaches highlighted in this book as a composite (or in total) because the practices described create what I propose to be an overall picture (or gestalt, so to speak) for effective classroom management. In other words, the whole is worth more than the sum of its parts, especially if those parts are viewed in isolation from one another. Furthermore, it is unlikely that you will find any one aspect of preventative practice highlighted to be, in and of itself, a panacea, silver bullet, or Holy Grail in terms of classroom management. Rather, the principles of practices described, when implemented in concert with one another, will help you establish and/or maintain a healthy learning environment (i.e., classroom climate) that will in its own way help you create a healthy balance between prevention and early and efficient intervention as it pertains to student behavior in your classroom.

As has been noted by many, as teachers we not only touch the future, but we also help create it as a result of our endeavors with our students. Our shared mission is to help our students learn and grow in a manner that enables each child to develop both academic as well as social and emotional (behavioral) competence. Given that you are reading this now, it is very likely that you already have an appreciation for the fact that student growth and learning involves a lot of things. One way in which I think about growth and learning is based on my experiences in preservice and graduate-level training of educators. In teacher preparation, we view growth and learning in students (current and future teachers) as relevant to their acquisition of the necessary knowledge, skills, and professional dispositions—or professionalism—to be effective teachers. I believe that knowledge, skills, and personal dispositions are relevant for students from preschool through the 12th grade. In particular, I suggest that as teachers we are important brokers of student growth in that we help our students learn problem-solving skills that lend themselves to both academic-intellectual and social-emotional situations. Helping our students become responsible contributing citizens as adults is a tall order, and as teachers what we do and how we do it have a direct impact on how our students grow and learn. Along these same lines, I would argue that the center of the learning process in our schools today continues to be the classroom—each individual classroom—and the level of achievement continues to be directly related to the degree of healthy mentoring relationships that is established between the classroom teacher and his or her students. Establishing an effective learning community within your classroom requires certain features to be present. The primary focus in Chapters 1 through 7 is to clearly 1) describe each of those preventative features, 2) help you see the interconnectedness of these preventative features, and 3) provide you with some guidance in approaches you can use to establish these preventative features holistically within your respective classroom setting. I will address each of these three areas of emphasis in Chapters 1 through 7 within the context of schools implementing PBIS as well as more traditional school settings. In Chapter 8 I will provide you with clear guidance on a continuum of time-efficient forms of early intervention that you can apply in your classroom if/when student misbehavior (behavioral error) occurs. Although reactive in nature, these forms of redirection procedures will be described within the context of preventative classroom management that, when implemented consistently in concert with your preventative approaches, can be effective and help you maximize your use of instructional time. Building on the prior chapters, Chapter 9 will provide you with easily understandable practices that you can use in the event that a particular student (or small group of students) fails to sufficiently respond to your use of the practices presented in Chapters 1 through 8. This chapter will provide specific descriptions along with illustrations of additional practices that you should find useful in working with such a student (or small group of students), who requires additional layers (or levels) of PBIS. These practices will, as well, be framed for use by teachers in both schools implementing PBIS and more traditional schools. In Chapter 10 I will help you address the question "So what if everything I have tried is still not sufficiently working?" In this chapter I will help orient you toward what is considered more individualized student-intensive approaches that should prove valuable in addressing the needs of students who require additional, layered PBIS. Of greatest value to you as a teacher, in this chapter, is practical guidance I will provide you with as to the array of support structures that you will likely need to access in order to realistically meet the needs of such a student while also continuing to meet the needs of all your other students. In the final chapter in this book I will provide you with guidance on how to pull everything together as described in previous chapters in a manner that is feasible and sustainable within your classroom.

I appreciate the time you are taking to read this book. We can all relate to (at least on occasion) feeling as though our time has been wasted on doing things that just don't seem to add up when it comes to making a difference with our students. I know firsthand that there is nothing more frustrating than to feel as though my time has been wasted on some task or activity that someone else has required me to do and that just does not seem to be directly connected to helping me better help my students. Time is an increasingly scarce commodity for all of us—in fact, I would argue the most precious commodity. As such, I thank you for your investment of time in reading this book and (most important) your time and energy in applying these principles of practice within your classroom.

> The center of the learning process in our schools today continues to be the classroom.

So Why Do Kids Act the Way They Do?

So why do kids act the way that they do? Boy, if there was a short answer to that question I would share it with you (as well as the world) and we could use the proceeds to solve the U.S. national debt. I believe the key to understanding or decoding student behavior lies, first and foremost, in understanding our actions and the nature of our behavior. In other words, it is helpful to think about our behavior and what influences how we act as a means to gaining a perspective about our students' behavior. I like to refer to this as thinking in the first person about our personal experiences in order to understand others. In reality, there are causal roots to why we act as we do within and across situations. As a general rule, our behavior, as well as our students' behavior, is not random (even though it may appear so from time to time). The interactive effect of both nature (or personal predispositions) and nurture (the things that happen to us or with us in our life circumstances) influences how each of us acts or reacts. Let me try to clarify what I mean by this interactive effect through a simple analogy. Think of a science experiment in which we will take two sets of fluids and mix them together. In this case, we will take hydrochloric acid, which will be contained in one beaker, and

H_2O (commonly known as water), which will be contained in a separate beaker. Each of these fluids, when isolated in separate beakers under stable conditions, is reasonably safe and innocuous to handle. However, when we take these two separate fluids and mix them together in to a third beaker, place a cork on that third beaker, and further agitate this mixture by shaking it up vigorously, we will likely experience a volatile effect (such as an eruption or explosion, so please do *not* try this home). This is somewhat akin to what happens when various factors in our lives come together within the ebb of flow of our daily experiences. For example, our actions and reactions are directly related to such interactive effects between what some would call our nature (genetic predisposition) and nurture (external influences on us within our environment). In other words, whether we are experiencing extreme stress or feeling relaxed and calm and subsequently act one way or another is not exclusively based on any one factor. Rather, both our feelings and our actions (behavior) are direct outgrowths of this interactive effect between nature and nurture. This is parallel to the chain of events our students experience daily, whether they are experiencing extreme stress and acting out or acting off task or feeling relaxed and calm and remaining focused and on task within the classroom. If your life is anything like mine, you have experienced a day in which things start out poorly when you leave for work and just seem to go downhill throughout the day in your classroom. Then, on returning home that same evening, you find that you are not as particularly resilient or

> The key to understanding or decoding student behavior lies, first and foremost, in understanding our actions and the nature of our behavior.

nurturing toward others as you might be following a better day in the field.

Sometimes those closest to you are the first to notice your "altered state" and may, in fact, comment on it, which can have an effect similar to throwing gas onto smoldering embers (or agitating hydrochloric acid and water under unstable conditions). It can be combustible to say the least. It is not that you love those at home any less at that moment in time—to the contrary, what you are likely looking for when stressed out is the unconditional love and support you have come to expect from those closest to you. When you are feeling exhausted and overwhelmed, however, the smallest thing can set you off, which can look ugly and make everyone involved feel unloved and underappreciated.

Further compounding the confusing nature of decoding behavior is how some kids just seem to be less inherently resilient and thus struggle to handle things as easily as other kids. For example, I am sure you have (at least) one kid who, regardless of what is thrown his or her way, is spontaneously reflexive and just always seems to land on his or her feet, much like a cat. Then there is _____ (you fill in the name here), who, despite all your best wishes, intentions, and good faith efforts to structure activities to improve his or her success in the classroom, just always seems to have the uncanny ability to respond to situations as if there was a conspiracy that was out to get him or her. This type of experience with your students, if you think about it in the first person in terms of your personal life experiences, is similar to situations that you may face with your colleagues (i.e., some may appear to be more inherently resilient daily compared with others). It seems that some people (kids and adults) have more natural insulation to fend off adverse factors in their respective worlds when compared with their peers.

So given all this, is it simply people's nature to do better when under stress as compared with others? Or is it an issue of nurture, in that we can engineer (alter) our situations and circumstances so that no one (student or colleague) is exposed to undue or unhealthy levels of stress? Nature (i.e., pathology) versus nurture (i.e., environment) is an age-old debate that has preoccupied many in the field and spawned some great movies, such as *Trading Places*, starring Dan Aykroyd and Eddie Murphy. In reality, rarely are the important issues of life as clear cut as asking the question, "Is it *X*, or is it *Y*?" (even though complex issues have a tendency to be portrayed in simplistic sound bites in our society today). In other words, both nature and nurture affect how we (or our students and colleagues) act at any given moment in time, and how we act or react may change across situations or over time. Therefore, in the classroom it looks as clear as mud on some given days, and this convoluted mess we call life can become even harder to understand when we allow ourselves to get trapped into playing the unproductive either-or game of nature versus nurture.

> Rarely are the important issues of life as clear cut as asking the question, "Is it *X*, or is it *Y*?"

So how do you go about making sense of all this? I mean, practically, what is a teacher supposed to do with all this in the classroom? Well, the key is in understanding two basic aspects of why kids act the way they do. First, all behavior (even challenging behavior by a given student) serves a purpose (technically referred to as a "function"), in that the behavior of concern helps the student address an unmet need as seen from his or her perspective. This is not to suggest that this, as a basic rule, legitimizes problem behavior. Rather, it is simply important to be able to decode the causal root behind why the student is acting in the manner that she or he is acting. The second concept to grasp about student behavior, coupled with decoding the function of behavior, is realizing that behavior is context related or situational. As such, the key to understanding why your kids act as they do and, in turn, helping these same kids grow and learn in your classroom, is to acknowledge the existence of what you cannot control (e.g., nature or pathology, including disability) while at the same time wisely investing your time and energy on the things you can directly influence (e.g., your classroom environment). The reality is that parents send the best kids that they have to school; they do not keep the better ones at home. You inherit, so to speak, the kids in your classroom at any given moment in time. As such, your job then becomes working with those kids in a manner that helps you meet them where they are in order to help them grow and learn over time. Understanding the nature of behavior and the importance of context can help you more efficiently understand why your students act as they do. In real estate, it has been suggested by many that selling a home is (mostly) about location, location, location. I would suggest that understanding student behavior, in a parallel sense, is (mostly) about context, context, context.

This notion of understanding context is equally relevant to you as a teacher within your school building as it is for you in understanding your students' behavior in your classroom. For example, it is highly likely that the value of understanding the function of student behavior in context is an inherent principle that is explicitly talked about among you and your colleagues if you happen to be teaching in a school that is implementing MTSS in the form of high-fidelity PBIS. This understanding serves as the bedrock for the array of preventative

> The reality is that parents send the best kids that they have to school; they do not keep the better ones at home.

approaches that are likely in place across what is commonly referred to as the universal level (Tier 1), targeted group level (Tier 2), and individual intensive level (Tier 3) at your school. However, if you happen to be teaching in a more traditional school system (that has not, as of yet, adopted PBIS), this notion of understanding student behavior in context may not be as explicit or prominent in the ebb and flow of operations within your school. This is not to suggest that the importance of this orientation to decoding student behavior is less important under these conditions. Rather, it is simply to draw to your attention to the notion that you may need to carefully think through how you will incorporate this belief not only in your actions within your classroom but also in your conversations with your colleagues, as it will be helpful to you in your endeavors with your students if increasingly other teachers in your school are embracing this same belief through their actions with their students.

As a teacher, you have a direct influence on the context for learning within your classroom. Although each student you have within your classroom may respond differently at different times, and some may be, in fact, more inherently resilient than others based on their life experiences prior to coming into your classroom, it is your work (the professional work of a teacher) to engineer your classroom so that all your students experience academic and behavioral success. Or, to quote Ginott,

> I have come to a frightening conclusion. I am the decisive element in the classroom. It is my personal approach that creates the climate. It is my daily mood that makes the weather. As a teacher, I possess tremendous power to make a child's life miserable or joyous. I can be a tool of torture or an instrument of inspiration. I can humiliate or humor, hurt or heal. In all situations it is my response that decides whether a crisis will be escalated or de-escalated, and a child humanized or de-humanized. (1972, pp. 15–16)

3

So How Do I Prevent Problem Behavior in My Classroom?

Your perspective, whether limited to your classroom or considered more broadly in life, directly affects how you interpret the events in your daily life. Developing perspective is a funny thing because it is a highly personalized experience and, much like art, interpreted by the eye of the beholder. Mark Twain has been credited with saying, "It ain't what you don't know that will get you in trouble, it's what you know for sure that just ain't so." Simply stated, a terminal degree of certainty is a dangerous thing to have about anything, most specifically about human behavior. The reality is that you will be unable to prevent inappropriate behavior from ever occurring in your classroom—unless either each of your students is Mother Teresa or your classroom has no students. Rather, what you can do is establish a few basic operating procedures that will enhance the learning environment in a way that can dramatically reduce the likelihood of both nuisance and problem behaviors.

Nuisance behaviors are those that in and of themselves are essentially inconsequential, such as a student's appearing fidgety and calling out to get your attention as opposed to raising his or her hand. It is often inconsequential behavior that should be ignored that, however, historically (or perhaps hysterically) has been known to get strong adverse reactions from teachers.

Yet problem behavior must be immediately stopped, and the student must be redirected to act in a more appropriate manner. For example, a student who is taking materials from another student must be told by the teacher, "Stop taking John's book and answer sheet. I want you to open your own book and do your work on your own." Perspective—*your* perspective to be specific—comes into play in understanding that inappropriate behaviors are not always equal and, realistically, you will never be able to control all student behavior. This may seem like an odd statement from someone providing guidance on classroom management, but it is an important concept to understand because it can dramatically affect your perspective and subsequent approach to classroom management.

One of my personal pet peeves with regard to classroom (behavior) management comes from the term *management*, which has become commonplace in the field. The very term implies this false notion of control in that it suggests that you will manage your students as if they were collectively nothing more than raw material to be organized within your classroom. I don't know about you, but I know I have enough difficulty managing my own behavior (especially on tough days), let alone managing anyone else's behavior. Now, having said this, there are things that you can manage that will help you have a direct positive effect on your students' behavior. The nature of these things that you can control (or at least greatly influence) ironically has less to do with your students' behavior and more to do with how you act or do not act daily in your classroom. I think a more accurate descriptor for classroom management is "Teacher Self-Management of

> Realistically, you will never be able to control all student behavior.

Instructional Practice in Group Settings," but this title is far too long and will understandably not catch on in the field. So I will use the term *classroom management* for simplicity's sake. Having said this, the important thing to keep in mind is not so much the term but the idea I am trying to communicate.

Developing a classroom management plan can appear daunting from the onset. I mean, there are so many things to take into account and plan for, and then you have to think about differentiation, adaptation, and possible modification to address unique student needs. The process of organizing the necessary resources to meet the unique needs of students who require varying levels of interventions and supports can be greatly facilitated through schoolwide adoption of MTSS/PBIS. However, whether your school is a PBIS school or school with a more traditional approach to addressing student behavioral issues, the need to provide an array of interventions and supports will be present. Although there are various aspects to consider when designing a game plan for your classroom, it helps keep things simple. For example, classroom management can be viewed as having two main themes: prevention and intervention. Understandably, it is easy to become preoccupied with searching for the illusive answer to the question "What do I do when a student does X?" Although you will need a set of standard operating procedures to efficiently and safely redirect inappropriate student behavior, the primary emphasis in effective classroom management is preventing problem behavior in the first place. A simple way to think about this is as follows: If you consider all the time that you will invest in managing student behavior in your classroom, a minimum of

80% of that behavior management time should be invested in preventative approaches. This so-called 80–20 split (80% prevention to 20% intervention) is generally accepted within the professional literature and is borne out daily within effective classrooms. Having noted this proportional weighting of your invested time in behavior management, there are precise tactics of teaching, or principles of practice, that are relevant to both prevention of as well as intervention with inappropriate student behavior. In particular, three specific preventative principles of practice serve as the foundation for effective classroom management that is within your immediate control as a classroom teacher. These three principles of practice are equally relevant whether you are teaching in a PBIS school or a more traditional school setting. Regardless of the type of classroom you operate (e.g., elementary, secondary, general, or special education), the following principles of practice are relevant for you:

> The primary emphasis in effective classroom management is preventing student problem behavior in the first place.

1. Rapport

2. Clear expectations

3. Reinforcement of expected behavior

These three approaches, when viewed in sum and in concert with one another, may best be visualized as a three-legged stool of prevention in which each component is somewhat interdependent on the presence of the other two components in order to bear the full weight of student behavior in your classroom.

The importance of establishing rapport with your students is (for the most part) a universally accepted

understanding in our schools today. Oddly enough, however, many teachers struggle daily with establishing rapport with all their students, especially those who appear
difficult to reach. In other words, we have somewhat of
an understanding as teachers regarding the importance
of connecting with our students, but as a field, we are
somewhat limited in our understanding of time-efficient,
systematic practices that we can use to establish rapport.
Thinking of your personal experiences in your classroom,
you most likely have established rapport with those students with whom you are most comfortable. More often than
not, these are the kids who provide you with a lot of reinforcement and are least likely to develop problem behavior
over time. As such, you likely would describe these kids
as your favorites. To be clear, and for the record, you are a
person first and a professional second. Therefore, you will
have favorites, and acknowledging this reality is an important first step to establishing rapport with your students
who are more difficult to reach. In our personal lives, we
get to choose those with whom we hang out and, to varying
extents, those whom we choose to avoid. As teachers, however, we don't have the luxury or right to pick and choose
those with whom we will
successfully establish rapport within our classrooms.

> You will have favorites, and
> acknowledging this reality
> is an important first step to
> establishing rapport with
> your students who are
> more difficult to reach.

You will likely find
yourself naturally gravitat-
ing toward your "favorite"
students (those kids who
provide you with a lot of positive reinforcement), as this
is human nature. I mean,
after all, we all would rather hang out with others who make
us feel good. The professional challenge is to 1) understand
this aspect of human nature and 2) reach out and connect
with those students who appear more distant from you in

terms of your personal comfort. Therefore, it is important to have a few time-efficient methods in your teacher "bag of tricks" that can help you establish a conducive level of rapport with each of your students—not just the ones toward whom you naturally gravitate. When it comes to effective teaching and rapport, the bottom line is that most kids don't care what you know as a teacher until they know that you really care about them as people (Albert, 1996). As such, it is helpful to regularly put into practice some simple rapport-building techniques that will help each of your students increasingly understand that you really do care about him or her on a personal level. If you are anything like most teachers that I know, you are a nurturing, fun-loving, and approachable person, but for a number of reasons, not all your students will see you in this light (at least not right away, and especially not those students who may appear to be most at risk to develop problem behavior). I will describe these rapport-building strategies in greater detail in Chapter 4, as they should prove helpful to you in reaching out and sufficiently connecting with all the kids in your classroom. Establishing a classroom environment conducive to learning (and developing rapport with each of your students) is enhanced by establishing a clear set of behavioral (social performance) expectations. In other words, rapport becomes a byproduct of your collective endeavors within the classroom, and although some teaching strategies can help you establish rapport, the effect of these tactics is greatly enhanced when used in tandem with clear social-performance expectations. Establishing (and teaching) clear and explicit performance expectations is a foundation in schools implementing PBIS. So if you are a teacher in a PBIS school you may likely have already experienced (at least to some degree) associated positive effects with your students beyond simple reduction in problem behavior through improved teacher–student inter-actions and relationships on many fronts, including aca-demic achievement. However, establishing clear and precise behavioral expectations is equally relevant for you, as well,

if you happen to be teaching in a more traditional school set-ting. Establishing expectations is all about developing a set of cultural norms within your classroom and ultimately about fostering social competence in all your students. To be clear, I am not talking about simply creating a list of rules or a list of "thou shalt nots." Rather, what I am referring to is identifying three to five broad expectations

> If you are anything like most teachers that I know, you are a nurturing, fun-loving, and approachable person, but for a number of reasons, not all your students will see you in this light.

toward which you will foster growth and progress with each of your students on an ongoing basis (e.g., "Be Respectful," "Be Responsible," "Be Safe"). Now you may be thinking, "This is too simple. I mean, it can't be that simple, can it?" Well, although there is more operational detail regarding expectations that you will need to address, starting at such a basic level steers you in the right direction. As the Roman philosopher Sen-eca noted, "If one does not know to which port one is sailing, no wind is favorable." Simply stated, you want to be sure that you are sailing in a direction that has some promising land ahead, instead of large ice-bergs to strike. Focusing your students' attention toward what you want them to do (instead of what you don't want them to do) is one of the most important first steps you can take.

Your second step is to focus attention on more opera-tionally defining these three to five expectations across important settings (and routines) throughout your given classroom day, thus creating not only a road map for behavior for your students but also a radar system for you to use in terms of reinforcing your students as they demonstrate appropriate behavior per your expectations. Establishing three to five broadly stated expectations (and subsequently defining these expectations across settings and routines with your students) also creates a healthy degree of predictability that helps your students realize that they can influence or have some degree of power over their own personal degree of success in your classroom (also known as locus of control). Steps and procedures to use to engage your students in the process of establishing behavioral expectations for your classroom are provided in Chapter 5.

> You want to be sure that you are sailing in a direction that has some promising land ahead, instead of large icebergs to strike.

Reinforcement is the third principle of practice in this three-legged stool of preventative approaches to classroom management. Look, we all know that we can attract more bees with honey or more ants with sugar. What I mean to say is that the best way to help students develop appropriate behavior is by being clear on expected behavior and, as the saying goes, "catching them being good." I know, I know, this is not a novel concept, but I never said I was going to share new, earth-shattering ideas with you. What I did say—even promise—was that I would help you develop a new perspective about classroom management that enables you to bring together (in full force) the basic aspects of prevention that will help you increasingly become a more effective educator. Simply stated, reinforcement serves as one of the three cornerstones of prevention (well, if you can have cornerstones associated with a three-legged stool).

Aristotle has been attributed with saying, "We are what we repeatedly do, therefore excellence is not an act—but a habit." Let me expand a bit on this notion: Each of us is going to form habits, and our habits, good or bad, develop over time in association with what we are reinforced for doing. Whether it is the habit of kindness or of rudeness, the principle of reinforcement (along with other factors) is in play. Instructionally, your goal becomes to help your students develop behavioral habits that are consistent with the social competencies you wish to see in your classroom. Ironically, you will help your students develop these positive habits as a direct result of your development of positive teaching habits that reflect these preventative approaches I am describing in this book. To this end, reinforcing your students for performing expected behavior should increasingly become the norm in your classroom. In addition, it is important to understand that there are various forms of reinforcement and that not all reinforcement procedures—and most certainly not all potential reinforcers used by you as a teacher—will be equal. As such, it is important to understand the nature of positive and negative reinforcement and to further appreciate that what is actually reinforcing is (much like interpreting a work of art) in the eyes of the beholder (or the one being reinforced). Make no mistake about it: Both positive and negative reinforcement are just that—forms of reinforcement to increase the likelihood of future recurrence of desired behavior. Positive reinforcement, however, is the bull's-eye, as you will see in greater detail in Chapter 6.

> Reinforcing your students for performing expected behavior should increasingly become the norm in your classroom.

Rapport, expectations, and reinforcement serve as three principles of practice in prevention of student problem behavior in your classroom. This is not to suggest that teaching practices such as active supervision of your students, conducting seamless transitions between activities in your classroom, or checking regularly for student understanding are unimportant—on the contrary, they are important. What I am suggesting, however, is that rapport, expectations, and reinforcement are the primary building blocks of effective classroom management. Each of these three principles of practice is important in its own right; however, the whole is worth far more than the sum of its parts. Regardless of the type of school setting in which you find yourself teaching, these preventative principles of practice should prove helpful to you with your students. These preventative approaches are consistent with universal level (Tier 1) approaches if you are teaching in a PBIS school. These same universal level approaches are, as well, equally applicable if you are teaching in a more traditional school setting. Given that, let's turn our attention to each of these principles of practice and, in turn, focus on specific teaching strategies along these same lines.

4

So How Close Should I Get with My Students?

I recall one particular teacher whom I had in high school who was simply brilliant in terms of his knowledge of the English language, breadth of understanding, and depth in description. Mr. Brice was incredibly gifted in the subject matter for which he had an understandable passion. Most (if not all) of his students (including yours truly), however, learned very quickly that Mr. Brice's passion clearly started and ended there. His approach to teaching could be summed up by saying he taught English to students rather than teaching students English. I, by no stretch of the imagination, would ever be accused of being gifted when it comes to the English language. At that stage in my life I couldn't tell you the difference between a dangling participle and a hanging curve ball other than what I knew from firsthand experience: If you are not careful, a hanging curve ball can knock your lights out. Despite my lack of expertise with the English language, I was a relatively decent student in high school and (for the most part) tried my best to succeed. I really struggled with Mr. Brice's class, however. At the time, I chalked it up to my shortcomings as a student, despite the fact that it seemed that everyone I knew also struggled with Mr. Brice, even the students in our honors program. In retrospect, what I have come to appreciate is that regardless of all the natural talent

Mr. Brice had in the English language, he clearly struggled with student language because he did not communicate (or at least appeared not to care to communicate) any interest in us as people first—let alone as students enrolled in his class.

I also recall vividly having another teacher from my high school days, Mr. Boyer, for American History and World Cultures. Mr. Boyer was a real hoot because he was always hanging around with his students (including myself) when he wasn't teaching, joking around, asking how we were doing, and going out of his way to help, even when it meant some extra time on his part. He clearly was a competent teacher in terms of both his knowledge of the subject matter and his understanding of students.

> Mr. Brice's approach to teaching could be summed up by saying he taught English to students rather than teaching students English.

What is amazing to me to this day is that I still have many vivid memories of not only the course content of American History and World Cultures but also the activities that we did during class time. Suffice it to say, Mr. Boyer's approach to teaching was that he taught students the value of history and an understanding of the importance of learning about other cultures as opposed to trying to force this knowledge on his students.

I have shared this bit of my personal experience as a student to set the stage for helping you understand the importance of establishing rapport with your students. Along these same lines, my goal in sharing this story is to help you develop some further insight into approaches that can work for you in your endeavors to teach your students the value of the curriculum as opposed to simply teaching the curriculum to your students. We all live our lives in the first person (seeing things through our personal eyes rather than our professional eyes), so a personal approach that is student centered (as opposed to subject centered) is in many ways a necessary first step in creating an effective learning environment in your classroom, where all your kids can thrive. The short of it is as follows: Regardless of prerequisite knowledge and/or interest in any given subject on the part of

> Mr. Boyer's approach to teaching was that he taught students the value of history and the importance of understanding other cultures as opposed to trying to force this knowledge on his students.

your students, your students are more likely to become increasingly motivated to learn and perform in your classroom if they understand that you have a genuine interest in them as people.

Creating a suitable level of rapport with your students will be, in many ways, an absolutely essential prerequisite for their achievement, especially those who appear the most difficult to reach. Establishing rapport does not mean that you have to become each student's best friend. Rather, it means gaining a closeness with each of your students in a way that positions you in each student's eyes as having his or her best interest at heart, even when the things you may be asking the student to do at a particular point in time are not high on his or her priority list. Such relationships are based on trust, which in turn helps with student motivation, requiring thoughtful tilling and planting of the soil (as in a garden). Classroom soil, so to speak, that is conducive to student learning does not simply produce growth on its own. Rather, growth is supported through your approach to teaching. Tilling this soil to build rapport is essential work whether you are teaching in a school using a

PBIS approach or a more traditional school setting. Make no mistake about it: Establishing rapport is a necessary building block for learning—especially with students who appear the hardest to reach.

So where do you start? How do you put in place the procedures that help you get and stay connected with your students? Well, with many of your students, the process will be quite easy; however, with a few, it will require a systematic approach. What typically happens is that you will—in a natural manner that will not be particularly conscious on your part—begin to develop rapport and a suitably close relationship with some of your kids sooner than others. Over the course of time, you will increasingly become closer with this subset of your students to the degree that—in all honesty—you might describe this group of students as your "favorites." As I said in Chapter 3, it is both natural and predictable that you will have favorites (which is not necessarily the same as showing favoritism). The good news is that you will not need to spend much (if any) time systematically thinking about establishing rapport with these students because these relationships will develop naturally. Rather, it is your students who are harder to reach who will be the ones with whom you need to employ a systematic process to establish rapport. In other words, these are the kids who do not, by their mere presence and actions in your classroom, provide you personally with the same degree of positive reinforcement as your "favorites." These are the students who are typically the hardest to reach, and yes, it is these kids in particular that you are paid as a professional to teach. This last statement

> Your students are more likely to become increasingly motivated to learn and perform in your classroom if they understand that you have a genuine interest in them as people.

may appear a bit blunt or harsh, but I do believe it to be true. Just as you will naturally develop favorites, you will also be prone to develop least favorites in relation to those kids whom you increasingly view as at risk for developing problem behavior.

In other words, the angst-ridden feelings that your students who are harder to reach may conjure up in the pit of your stomach will likely require you

> Your students who are harder to reach will be the ones with whom you need to employ a systematic process to establish rapport.

to increase your focus on your self-management skills so that you consistently act in a professional manner—that is, in order to defy your basic human instinct to increasingly avoid interactions with others who do not provide you with a lot of positive reinforcement (I mean who wants to— out of choice—be around others who don't make you feel good?). You should thoughtfully and consistently increase your use of systematic procedures that help you connect with students, in order to nurture rapport with your students who are at risk for developing behavioral problems.

There are two primary aspects to building rapport. First, we need to look at the precise steps or actions (observable behaviors) involved with getting close to your students. Second, we need to look at the application of these steps and procedures (observable behaviors) in the context of suitable situations within which to use these rapport-building procedures. Your use of these rapport-building procedures is easily applicable in most school settings.

Rapport building, as with any other form of teaching activity, can be broken down into a series of steps through task analysis. The component steps represent links within an entire chain of events. In this sense, the following sequence of steps is involved when

Table 4.1. Steps in building rapport

Demonstrate close proximity (move toward the student and be within arm's reach).

Demonstrate age-appropriate touch (e.g., shake hands, high-five).

Demonstrate appropriate facial expressions (reflect the nature of the situation).

Demonstrate appropriate tone of voice (voice matches situation).

Demonstrate appropriate body language (e.g., appear relaxed, keep arms open, be attentive, look at student).

Ask open-ended positive questions (e.g., "What are you doing after school?" "How do you do so well in your track meets?" "What was your favorite part of the movie?"). If you ask questions that require one-word answers, that is what you will likely get from a student with whom you are not already close.

Listen while the student is speaking. Ideally, talk less than the student (try not to interrupt or abruptly change the topic).

Demonstrate the use of empathy statements. Act like a mirror and reflect the child's feelings by expressing your understanding and caring.

Ignore nuisance behavior and let the little stuff slide (but not problem behavior if it surfaces).

Stay cool throughout the process, which can be easier said than done.

Source: Latham (1999).

systematically building rapport with your students (see Table 4.1).

The steps associated with rapport building may also be viewed as component parts of basic interpersonal communication skills (in their simplest sense). As such, this task analysis may also be used as a form of curriculum when providing direct instruction to particular students who require help in acquiring basic social interaction skills.

At first glance, understanding the mechanics (the observable behaviors) of building rapport appears relatively easy. Nervousness and anxiety complicate applying these steps because it may feel risky to reach out in this manner to a student (or small number of students) from whom you are already feeling distant. Having a clear understanding of these steps, as simple as they may appear, can be reassuring to you when you begin to make your proverbial leap of faith toward a few particular students. Beyond your basic understanding of the mechanics of building rapport, it is also important to provide you with some guidance about appropriate situations in which to employ these procedures.

To explain the process of reaching out, think about some experiences in your personal life. Specifically, think back to some point in time when you were at some social gathering (e.g., holiday party, hanging out with friends). Let's say you are at this event where you know some, but not all, of the guests. Suddenly, you see this person whom you do not know but would really like to get to know (call it physical attraction if you want). Now, if you are like most people I know, even though you may think you're courageous, you would not just take the risk and "go for it" by directly (and impulsively) approaching this person. In reality, you would probably give some time and thought to a number of things before making your first overture. Specifically, you would likely 1) think about how to approach him or her, 2) talk with someone at the event that you already know who happens to know him or her, 3) think about what types of things are of interest to him or her to start a conversation, and 4) find a natural way (so it does not seem contrived) to bump into him or her to have a conversation, and so forth. In other words, you likely give many things a lot of thought (even if it is within a very short period of time) *before* you make your approach. You are concerned about these things for a number of reasons, which can generally be summarized as "you never get a second chance to make a first impression."

Now, with this as a mental context, think about a particular kid (or two) with whom you need to develop a more conducive level of rapport. You will want to give serious thought to his or her interests (e.g., music, sports, art). Furthermore, you will need to think about appropriate situations (conducive settings) in which you can constructively get some level of dialogue started with him or her regarding these interests. What I am talking about here is what I like to describe as "breaking the ice" and strategic use of "ice breakers." The key is that you need some way to engage the student in a conversation about his or her interests within a safe/targeted situation in order to start the process of building rapport.

Now to do this, you will likely have to give some time and thought (conduct some research, so to speak) to figure out what interests to tap into as well as what situations (conducive settings) to target. You are looking for opportunities within the student's typical daily routine that are noninstructional in nature that would lend themselves to social interaction (e.g., during homeroom or lunch, transitions between classes, or transitions within your classroom) so that your interactions are not dependent on the student being successful with any given academic task (at least at that moment in time). You want to provide free access to your attention (noncontingent) in this sense.

Along these same lines, it is important to understand that you can use rapport-building procedures in a couple of ways, either in a one-to-one situation with the focus student or in small-group situations using other students, with whom your rapport is stable, as social brokers with the student of concern. There is no one right way that is necessarily better than the other to start the process. My best advice is to pick one that you feel the most comfortable with or one that you are the least uncomfortable with as you plan your approach. Ideally, you will find yourself using a combination of these approaches as your confidence with your students grows.

For example, Jimmy is a student from whom you are feeling increasingly distant. You have done some investigative work and found out that he is really into video gaming. Based on your detective work you found out that he is a part of the video-gaming club at the middle school in which you teach. Knowing this, you begin to look for opportunities (short snippets of time or windows of opportunity) during club time at school as well as during the common lunch period that you share with Jimmy to ask his advice on video game purchases for a friend's kid. You continue to build on these interactions by exploring ways to have additional brief conversations with Jimmy during transitions over the course of a couple weeks to the point at which, after a month or so, Jimmy occasionally goes out of his way to find you to ask if your friend bought the games and if his son liked them.

> You never get a second chance to make a first impression.

The final point on applying rapport-building strategies is to understand that a given student from whom you feel distant will unlikely open up to you after your first attempt to break the ice. Sometimes it will happen, but this is more the exception to the rule. It is more likely that incrementally, over time, a given student will gradually allow you to get closer to him or her as his or her comfort level with you grows. In other words, as with most relationships, it will take time to evolve. The key in using rapport-building procedures is to use them whenever and wherever you find (or can create) the opportunity. You will need to do this systematically with students from whom you feel distant—those who are potentially at risk in your classroom. Although you will not be able to predict how long it will take with any given student, the one thing you can have confidence in is that the relationship will likely improve over the course of time. Also, understand that unlike the personal social interaction that I asked you to reflect on earlier, your intent with any particular student with any given rapport-building encounter is not for a long-term interaction at that point in time. Rather, rapport-building procedures applied in this fashion usually take as little time as 15 seconds up to 2 minutes, depending on the situation. Thus the key is finding easily accessible non-instructional times throughout the typical school day as previously described to apply these procedures. In other words, pick the low-hanging fruit in terms of easy and frequent access rather than identifying less frequently available situations and or settings (e.g., after-school events). Therefore, the key (or power) is in the cumulative effect over time based on your repeated interactions with your students.

> Over time, a given student will gradually allow you to get closer to him or her as his or her comfort level with you grows.

Now, as important as rapport-building procedures are—and make no mistake about it, they are important—they represent only one of the proverbial legs of the three-legged stool of prevention. In other words, establishing a good working rapport with all your students will get you so far, but by itself it will be insufficient in terms of classroom management. It is important to combine such strategies to connect with your students by establishing clear and reasonably high behavioral expectations in your classroom. As such, let's turn our attention to establishing expectations with your students—the second leg of our three-legged stool of effective classroom management.

5

So How Do I Go About Establishing Expectations in My Classroom?

It is helpful to be familiar with the past as we forge toward the future. As such, I thought you might enjoy a quick glimpse in the rearview mirror into the past of school discipline and, in particular, codes of conduct from the early 1900s (see Table 5.1). I find the behavior concerns (and corresponding consequences) from this era whimsically of interest. In particular, if "boys and girls playing together" is worth four lashes, then it really makes me wonder what they had in mind in terms of "misbehaving girls" (ten lashes). I mean, my imagination is really running wild on this one. What if those girls were playing cards while misbehaving around the creek, mill, or barn? Anyway, beyond the humor in looking into the past, there is one important takeaway from our disciplinary history. The behaviors noted (although reflective of that particular era) emphasize an exclusively punitive approach to establishing behavior expectations. In other words, what is provided is simply a list of proverbial "thou shalt nots," with varying degrees of retribution for various offenses. Although one should

Table 5.1. School discipline circa 1900

Offense	Punishment
Boys and girls playing together	4 lashes
Fighting at school	5 lashes
Quarreling at school	5 lashes
Gambling and betting at school	4 lashes
Playing cards at school	10 lashes
Climbing each foot over 3 feet up a tree	1 lash
Telling lies	7 lashes
Telling tales out of school	8 lashes
Giving each other ill names	3 lashes
Swearing at school	8 lashes
Misbehaving girls	10 lashes
Drinking spirituous liquor at school	8 lashes
Wearing long fingernails	2 lashes
Misbehaving to people on the road	4 lashes
Boys going to girls' play places	3 lashes
Girls going to boys' play places	3 lashes
Coming to school with dirty face and hands	2 lashes
Calling each other liars	4 lashes
Wetting each other while washing at playtime	2 lashes
Scuffling at school	4 lashes
Going or playing about the creek	6 lashes
Doing mischief about the barn or mill	7 lashes

Sources: Gatto (n.d.); ThinkQuest (n.d.).

always look at the nature of the times in question when considering historical aspects of schools and society, it is interesting that many classroom-management approaches in schools today could also be described as a modern-day list of "thou shalt nots." Although we could change items such as "scuffling at school" to "no bullying," the emphasis of such approaches is on what *not* to do rather than on a more constructive approach that outlines what to do.

Both the literature and experience tell us that the most effective way to influence student behavior is by being clear about what you want your students to do, directly teaching the expected behavior and providing reinforcement to your students when they do it. Although it is certainly relevant to have naturally occurring consequences for student misbehavior (short of the "lashes," of course, regardless of the era), such consequences are most effective when delivered in concert with high levels of positive reinforcement for expected behavior. For example, it is certainly understandable that we do not want to see students bullying other students in our classrooms. Having said this, however, the most effective way to minimize the likelihood of such problem behavior is by investing our time and attention on providing explicitly clear expectations for alternative appropriate behaviors (e.g., being respectful toward others) and teaching and subsequently reinforcing our students for meeting these same expectations. On the surface, this may seem like nothing more than a game of semantics, but when you look at this in the larger scheme of classroom management, it is as different as sailing east compared with sailing west. For the record, I am not naïve, nor am I proposing that you take what might be understandably dismissed as a *Walden Two* approach to classroom management (in which life is beautiful all the time and we sit around

> Although it is certainly relevant to have naturally occurring consequences for student misbehavior, such consequences are most effective when delivered in concert with high levels of positive reinforcement for expected behavior.

giving group hugs and singing "Kumbaya"). Look, we all need to have specific procedures and consequences for undesired behavior in place in our classrooms. The key to preventing problem behavior from occurring in the first place, however, is establishing clear expectations for desired behavior, directly teaching the expected behavior, and reinforcing our students as they perform those same behaviors regularly.

Establishing student behavior expectations in the classroom (and schools in general) has received much attention over the years. Increasingly schools have been expanding the application of scientifically validated approaches to enhance the academic, social, and emotional learning of students. The multitiered framework known as PBIS that is being implemented in thousands of schools across the country and abroad is one of these scientifically validated approaches. Establishing clear expectations is, without question, one of the cornerstones in schools implementing PBIS. However, and not surprisingly, there continues to be discussion in the field about implementing expectations that make sense and are feasible for any classroom teacher—whether in a PBIS school or a more traditional school setting. In other words, it is important to breathe life into what the research literature suggests in a manner that is both useful and user friendly. Table 5.2 reflects the fundamental aspects of establishing expectations so that the students in your classroom increasingly demonstrate social competence, which also helps you set the stage for developing academic competence with each of your students as a result of increased achievement in your classroom.

As the old saying goes, one needs to know the bull's-eye if one is to be held accountable for hitting the mark. As such, you need to start by identifying three to five (no more, no less) broad behavior expectations that encompass the types

Table 5.2. Fundamental aspects of establishing clear behavioral expectations in the classroom

Select three to five positively stated, broad behavioral expectations.

Identify your highest priority settings and/or routines within which you anticipate the greatest likelihood of student problem behavior.

Operationally define each of your three to five expectations across each of your identified settings/routines by asking yourself, "What would my students look and sound like if they were being successful?" Try to engage your students in the process.

Post your behavioral expectations prominently in your classroom.

Provide initial instruction concerning your expectations at the start of the year, and provide booster sessions periodically throughout the school year.

Reinforce your students on a regular basis for appropriate behavior—catch them being good.

Have clear, systematic (and reasonable) consequences for student problem behavior.

of social behaviors you desire in your students (e.g., Be Responsible, Be Respectful, Be Ready). There is not an exclusive set of expectations in the literature for use in your classroom; the key is to identify expectations that make sense to you in your specific classroom. Have fun with acronyms and mnemonics as you see appropriate. For example, some teachers have used the "Three Bees" noted previously and subsequently have employed a bumblebee motif throughout the year in their classrooms. Other teachers have successfully used different sets of expectations to create phrases such as STARS (*S*trive to succeed, *T*ry your best, *A*chieve to your potential, *R*espect yourself and others, and *S*afety first) or SOAR (*S*afe, *O*rganized, *A*ttentive, and *R*esponsible). Obviously, if you are teaching in a PBIS school, you will want to be sure to use the already identified three to five expectations that your school has targeted. You will, of course, have greater latitude in identifying your three to five expectations if you are teaching in a more traditional school setting that has not (at least to date) adopted a PBIS approach.

Identifying your broad, positively stated expectations is the first step in establishing student behavior expectations in your classroom. The next step is to think about your classroom and the types of activities you will have the students do within your classroom. This second step in the process of establishing your expectations for your classroom is generally the same regardless of whether you teach in a PBIS or more traditional school setting. As you think about your classroom, think about both physical settings (locations) and routines within your classroom that have historically produced the greatest likelihood of student behavioral errors. You may be able to draw from your database (e.g., Schoolwide Information System [SWIS]) if you are teaching in a PBIS school. If not, rely on your intuitive recollection based on your instructional experiences in your classroom. If you are new to your classroom this year, then think about the types of situations that might predictably have the greatest likelihood to create either confusion or problem behavior in your students. In other words, what situations/contexts are most likely to give you the biggest headaches in terms of classroom management? Specifically, think about physical locations within your room (e.g., coat area, supply areas, work stations, and lab areas) in combination with high frequency routines associated with your expectations (e.g., entering and exiting the classroom, getting to work right away on independent or group work, asking for help when needed, sharing materials and supplies during group tasks). Identifying four or five of your highest priority settings and routines is a necessary next

> It is important to breathe life into what the research literature suggests in a manner that is both useful and user friendly.

step to breathe operational life into your expectations. I encourage you to use the matrix depicted in Figure 5.1 for planning purposes once you have identified your expectations as well as your priority settings/routines within your classroom (a larger, reproducible version of this form is also included in the Appendix and online).

Once you have plugged your broad expectations into the left-hand side of this planning matrix and your priority settings/routines across the top, you are ready to take the final step (prior to planning and providing direct instruction) in establishing your behavior expectations. The next step is to operationally define each of your expectations across each of your targeted (priority) settings/routines. The most important reason for this is that appropriate behavior will likely look different from setting to

EXPECTATIONS PLANNING MATRIX

Expectations	Context 1:	Context 2:	Context 3:	Context 4:
Expectation 1:				
Expectation 2:				
Expectation 3:				
Expectation 4:				
Expectation 5:				

Figure 5.1. Depiction of the expectations planning matrix.

setting or routine to routine (e.g., being responsible while doing independent seat work such as taking a test looks and sounds different from being responsible while doing group work). A simple way to think about operationally defining any given expectation is simply to ask yourself, "What would my students look and sound like if they were meeting this expectation within this setting/routine?" Furthermore, along these same lines, asking this question significantly increases the likelihood of operationally defining expected behaviors that are desirable as opposed to creating a modern-day version of "thou shalt nots." To help you in this regard, I encourage you to apply what has been commonly referred to as the "dead man test" to any behavior expectation that you establish in your classroom. Once you have defined an expectation within each setting/routine, ask yourself, "Could a dead person perform this expectation as stated?" If you answer "yes" (e.g., a dead person excels at "no pushing or shoving others"), then go back to the drawing board because your behavior expectation is in need of repair. Applying the "dead man test" can help you minimize the likelihood of defining your broad expectations in terms of statements such as "no running, no stealing, no fighting, no swearing," all the way up through "no boys going into girl play spaces." In other words, if a dead person can perform the expectation, then it is probably not a particularly useful behavior expectation in terms of serving as an expectation for instruction and reinforcement. Applying the "dead man test" in this manner can also help you reduce the likelihood of awkward moments with

> A simple way to think about operationally defining any given expectation is to ask yourself, "What would my students look and sound like if they were meeting this expectation within this setting/routine?"

that one kid who always seems to be able to find the gray space in lists of rules when presented in the form of "thou shalt nots" by saying, "That wasn't on the list of things we couldn't do." I know, I know— each of us always seems to have one kiddo like this in the classroom who can drive you crazy to the point of needing to fight the urge on a particularly difficult day to say something to the effect of, "Well, binding your hands and feet is not on the list either. Shall I just go ahead and chain you all to your desks now?" But of course the cooler, more professional side of your brain kicks in to help you refrain from making such a statement (at least out loud)—thus the need for "teacher self-management of instructional practice in group settings." Anyway, I think you get my point in this regard. The Appendix at the end of this book includes examples of behavior expectation matrices from various elementary, middle, and high school classrooms to help get you started.

> If a dead person can perform the expectation, then it is probably not a particularly useful behavior expectation in terms of serving as an expectation for instruction or reinforcement.

We all generally accept the notion that good instructional practices engage students actively as learners in our classrooms. As such, actively engaging your students in the process of defining your expectations across setting/ routines is highly encouraged. This is, of course, equally applicable in classrooms within PBIS schools and more traditional school systems. Although there are a number of good reasons to consciously consider doing this, the two most important reasons are that by doing so you 1) are actually preteaching the expectations as a result of the process of asking the kids to help you define the expectations and 2) increase the initial degree of "buy-in" (motivation) as you are providing increasing degrees of locus of control for each of your students by having them help you define the expectations within the parameters you have provided. This, much like the initial selection of your broad expectations, can take on many forms. The key is to find the way with which you are most comfortable in engaging your students in the process. For example, at the beginning of the school year, have each student come up with some privately developed operational definitions and then have students do some pair-share work leading up to a large-group discussion in your classroom. Another way is simply to engage your students in structured large-group discussion on the first day of school and (depending on the age and nature of your students) have them develop skits and/or demonstrations comparing and contrasting the appropriate versus inappropriate ways in which to act in the classroom. Be sure to have your kids apply the "dead man" test for all the previous noted reasons—plus it can add to the fun in your classroom! Your professional judgment, of course, will serve as your primary navigational device along these same lines. The key is that you can engage your students in the process and actually have fun based on what you believe is the best way to go in your classroom.

As with any aspect of effective teaching, it is important to provide clear expectations for student performance in concert with directly teaching the behavior expectations coupled with reinforcement for student performance of your expectations on an ongoing basis. It is important to post your established behavior expectations clearly to support your students to collectively act in a manner that creates a culture of social competence within your classroom. This is, of course, the exact same approach used in nonclassroom settings in your building if you teach in a PBIS school (e.g., prominently displaying your agreed-upon three to five expectations in such locations as the hallways, cafeteria, and other common spaces). A culture of social competence will develop in your classroom over time as your students are reminded by the public posting of the expectations in tandem with your direct instruction and reinforcement procedures and with your students prompting appropriate social behavior from one another regularly. Public posting will also serve as a visual reminder for you to "catch your kids being good" for the purpose of rein-

> It is important to post your established behavior expectations clearly to support your students to collectively act in a manner that creates a culture of social competence within your classroom.

forcement, which leads us to the third leg of the proverbial three-legged stool of effective classroom management: reinforcement procedures.

6

So How Hard Is It to Use Reinforcement in My Classroom?

So what is reinforcement, and, in particular, how should reinforcers be used in the classroom? There are two types of reinforcement: positive and negative. Understanding the similarities and differences between these two forms of reinforcement will set the stage for effectively selecting and using reinforcers with students in your classroom as a part of your management system.

By definition (and yes, it will be necessary to use some jargon for a bit, so please bear with me), *positive reinforcement* is the presentation of a desired stimulus contingent on the performance of a desired behavior in order to increase the likelihood of future recurrence of that same desired behavior (e.g., verbally praising a student, presuming that he or she finds verbal praise desirable, after he or she demonstrated an expected social skill, such as being responsible in your classroom). In a compatible yet contrasting manner, *negative reinforcement* is the removal of an undesired stimulus upon the performance of a desired behavior in order to increase the likelihood of future recurrence of that same desired behavior. For example, if a teacher needs to escort a student from class to class because he or she is having problems during class transitions, then once the student shows improved behavior, the teacher can stop escorting the student. Presuming that the student prefers to not be escorted by the teacher, the removal of the escort is negative reinforcement.

> Understanding the similarities and differences between positive and negative reinforcement will set the stage for effectively selecting and using reinforcers with students in your classroom as a part of your management system.

It is important for all of us as teachers to understand the similarities and differences of positive and negative reinforcement. As a high school special education teacher supporting students with disabilities within inclusive classroom settings there were many different students for whom I shared responsibility with other high school teachers. One who comes immediately to mind was Sam, who was in 11th grade. One of the expectations established with Sam was for him to constructively use his assigned study hall time at the end of the day (2 days per week) to begin completion of his homework assignments. Sam historically was inconsistent (at best) with homework completion. Now, in light of this expectation, it would have been possible for me to get Sam to work on his homework during a given study hall through frequent verbal reminders every time I would see Sam throughout the day leading up to study hall (which Sam would likely have viewed as "nagging"). Furthermore, if this became the predominant way in which I tried to get Sam to meet this expectation, he may have complied in the short run (for that given study hall), but this would likely have not been sustainable behavior change, as it would be mostly dependent on me "nagging" Sam daily. I may have also inadvertently undercut my ability to build rapport over the long run as a result of being increasingly viewed by Sam as a "nag"—someone to be avoided. Rather, by building in positive reinforcement procedures (simple verbal acknowledgment provided privately with Sam with periodic proactive prompts, short of nagging) Sam increasingly began taking his homework materials with him to study hall as well as gradually completing greater amounts of homework regularly. The bottom line is that positive reinforcement (in a general sense) is the more constructive way to go in terms of reinforcement.

Now, make no mistake about it, both positive and negative reinforcement procedures are just that: reinforcement procedures. In other words, negative reinforcement is not punishment. Rather, both forms of reinforcement have the result of increasing the likelihood of desired behavior. Positive reinforcement, however, is the predominant procedure to employ in your classroom for a number of reasons. Most important, it increases the likelihood of desired behavior in a way that also helps you build and maintain rapport with your students. In other words, as in my example with Sam, you do not want to jeopardize or trade off your rapport to simply see dull compliance in the short run as a result of using negative reinforcement on a regular or increasing basis (which can become a very slippery slope). Used sparingly and interspersed with a lot of positive reinforcement, negative reinforcement can be useful, but it should come with a warning label that advises all of us to use it with extreme caution.

> The bottom line is that positive reinforcement (in a general sense) is the more constructive way to go in terms of reinforcement.

Having noted the relationship between positive and negative reinforcement and having learned that positive reinforcement is really the name of the classroom management game, it is important to identify things such as praise, privileges, and attention that your students enjoy.

First consider the reinforcing nature of your time and attention, as this is readily at your disposal. By this, I am not suggesting that attention is a universal reinforcer that will work with each student in all situations. Rather, I am suggesting that you will likely find that your attention will serve as one of your most easily accessible and (perhaps) powerful forms of reinforcement. The key to selecting reinforcers is figuring out your students' interests. Some kids respond well to public praise for performance and other kids respond well to private praise, whereas others may respond better to a combination of public and private praise. The challenge comes in understanding your students and figuring out what makes each one tick (so to speak). You will likely find that acknowledging appropriate behavior in the form of praise is a relatively cost-effective form of reinforcement that you can easily use daily in your classroom. You can always build in additional systematic forms of reinforcement in your classroom (e.g., use of tangible slips of paper or coupons in the form of a token economy) as the nature of your classroom and your teaching style urges you. This can easily be done in a manner compatible with other forms of lottery-type drawings that may already be in operation if you happen to be teaching in a PBIS school. However, this can also be accomplished in your classroom if you happen to be teaching in a more traditional school setting. It is essential to pair precise verbal praise that makes clear to the student the action that is

> You do not want to jeopardize or trade off your rapport simply to see dull compliance in the short run as a result of using negative reinforcement on a regular or increasing basis (which can become a very slippery slope).

being acknowledged along with other forms of naturally occurring reinforcers regardless of teaching in a PBIS or more traditional school setting.

One of the more common uses of reinforcement procedures involves applying the Premack Principle, in which access to something (stimulus) that is desired is made contingent on the performance or use of something (stimulus) that is less preferred in such a manner that the likelihood of increased performance or use of the preferred thing (stimulus) becomes more predictable over time. Another way of stating this same principle of reinforcement is that a more probable activity can be used to reinforce a less probable activity.

> Acknowledging appropriate behavior in the form of praise is a relatively cost-effective form of reinforcement that you can easily use daily in your classroom.

Given this definition of the Premack Principle, do you feel confident enough in your understanding to start to apply it in your classroom daily? Your initial reaction to the previous descriptions of the Premack Principle may be similar to my initial reaction when a mentor exposed me to these same descriptions—"What a bunch of gobbledy gook. Why can't people just say things in plain language?" The definition I have given, although technically accurate, leaves much for translation and does little to help you gain a practical understanding of this important concept. Perhaps a more user-friendly way to define this principle of reinforcement is to rename it the "Meal Time Rule." The "Meal Time Rule" is familiar to parents and children alike: "You can have dessert after you eat all your vegetables." The Premack Principle, although important, is nothing more than having an understanding that in life sometimes you have to do one thing (that is not necessarily something you enjoy doing for its own sake, such as eating your vegetables) in order to gain access to another thing (that which you prefer, such as dessert). Now, some may say this is nothing more than bribery and that it is manipulative in nature. I guess in a narrow sense it is, but if this is true, then so too is much of life because gaining access to things that we prefer is often somewhat contingent on our performance of other things (e.g., as much as I enjoy teaching, I do get a paycheck every 2 weeks that I highly value). The reality is that the Premack Principle is in play every day in each of our lives. In other words, it is not just something that is used by you (or me) as a teacher but also a part of everyday life for each of us because we have all had some degree of experience with this principle of reinforcement. Beyond the "Meal Time Rule," Table 6.1 provides examples of the Premack Principle in action.

> The Premack Principle, although important, is nothing more than having an understanding that in life sometimes you have to do one thing in order to gain access to another thing.

Now, with your current understanding about the principle of reinforcement (and the nature of reinforcers), let's turn our attention to the pragmatics of using reinforcement in your classroom regularly. Providing structured opportunities to respond (OTRs) becomes essential to establishing a positive learning environment in your classroom. Student engagement serves as the foundation of constructing opportunities to deliver positive reinforcement to students when they meet expectations. Experience (and the literature) clearly indicates that students tend to demonstrate fewer behavioral problems and improved academic achievement when teachers provide more OTRs within the ebb and flow of classroom instruction. So the more frequently you can have your students directly engaged through responding to questions the

Table 6.1. Examples of the Premack Principle in everyday life

Less desired behavior	More desired behavior
If you share your toys with others	Then others will be more likely to share their toys with you
If you appropriately say "please," "thank you," and "I am sorry"	Then you will increase your number of friends in the classroom
If you organize and complete your assigned work promptly	Then you will earn higher grades and associated privileges
If you consistently come home by curfew	Then you can stay out until 11:00 p.m. on the weekend
If you consistently drive responsibly	Then you may have access to the family car when needed
As a person in a relationship, if you will simply be still and listen (as opposed to trying to solve the problem) when your significant other is going off (sharing) about something that upset him or her that day at work	Then _____ (I am confident that you can fill in this blank)

more readily available opportunities will occur to provide contingent positive reinforcement to your students.

One common misunderstanding about reinforcing student behavior is that many teachers feel that in order to be fair, everyone should get the same amount of reinforcement (e.g., number of instances of verbal praise, high-fives, or the delivery of tokens). Simply put, fairness does not necessarily mean that everyone gets the same thing at the same time. Rather, fairness really means (especially in the learning process within your classroom) that everyone gets what he or she needs with the understanding that needs will vary from student to student and that these needs change over time and across different situations. To help you understand this point, I will paraphrase Dr. Richard Lavoie (presenter of the F.A.T. [Frustration, Anxiety, and Tension] City workshop) through the following illustration.

Suppose that I am providing a professional development training session at a local school when, suddenly, a teacher by the name of Susan slumps over in her chair, falls to the floor in full cardiac arrest, and appears to have stopped breathing. How ludicrous would it be if I said, "Susan, I would really like to help you out here. I mean, I know CPR and first aid. In fact, I am certified in both. I could save your life, but I just don't have time to give everyone in the classroom CPR or mouth-to-mouth resuscitation. It just wouldn't be fair for me to give it to you and not to the rest of these nice folks in attendance here today. So although I don't like it any more than you do, I guess you are on your own." You see, the issue of fairness is really about providing access to what students need so that those same students are in a position to benefit from instruction. This, in fact, is the underlying rationale behind larger-school and community-sponsored endeavors such as breakfast programs at school, free and reduced lunch endeavors, and other forms of extended school services such as after-school child care. To reiterate, fairness does not necessarily mean that everyone gets the same thing at the same time. Rather, fairness really means (especially in the learning process within your classroom) that each student gets what he or she needs with the understanding that personal needs will vary from student to student and that these needs change over time and across different situations.

> Fairness really means that everyone gets what he or she needs with the understanding that needs will vary from student to student and that these needs change over time and across different situations.

Another way to think about differences of need in your classroom in terms of reinforcement (and your ability to differentiate your use of reinforcement to meet each of your student's needs) is through the following analogy. Differentiating reinforcement procedures among students is like differentiating your eating patterns based on your level of hunger. I mean, you and I eat (in general) only when we are hungry (with perhaps the exception of holiday gluttony). For example, let's say you and a friend are attending my in-service training. You have just come from lunch where you were able to order your favorite food from a local eatery, and you are stuffed. Another friend, however, missed lunch today due to an appointment. So I kindly offer her some peanut butter crackers that I happen to have in my travel bag. I do not offer you the same. As long as you don't feel that my failure to offer you some crackers was mean-spirited in nature, it's unlikely that you're going to get too upset that your colleague was offered something to eat and you were not because you currently feel full and you know (and you know that I am also aware that) your friend is hungry. Your friend has a need for something to eat at this moment in time, whereas you do not. This doesn't mean that you will never be hungry again. Rather, you simply are not hungry at this moment in time. Thinking about differentiating your practice of reinforcement in this way can be very useful in that 1) it helps you understand that what is reinforcing at a given moment in time is relative to the person being reinforced and 2) it can be liberating (as a teacher) to understand that the goal is not to deliver the exact same amount of reinforcement (e.g., verbal praise) from student to student as if you were a human candy dispenser or gumball machine.

> What is reinforcing at a given moment in time is relative to the person being reinforced.

Now, given what I have shared with you thus far about reinforcement, and in particular about positive reinforcement, you have to be thinking, "So how do I figure out what is the right amount of reinforcement to provide to my students? I mean, in a practical sense, how do I make this work in my classroom?"

Well, first, I encourage you to understand that there is not some preset number of times that reinforcement should be delivered on any given day and instead to think about your reinforcement procedures in terms of what I like to describe as a range of proportionality. By this I mean that you want to aim to provide four instances of positive reinforcement for any given student's appropriate social behavior for every one time you find yourself giving that same student corrective feedback for problem behavior. This is what is meant in the educational field by achieving the infamous 4:1 ratio. Now, in this sense, everyone gets access to the same thing (your achievement of this 4:1 ratio). What is different from student to student may be the time interval within which the 4:1 ratio is achieved based on each student's needs.

Let's say you have three particular kids in your second-grade classroom who, for a variety of reasons to your mind's eye, are increasingly becoming distant from you (despite your efforts to increase rapport-building opportunities with each of them). In a parallel sense you find yourself correcting problem behavior with each of these three kids to a greater extent than the rest of your class. Let's say Jane seems to warrant corrective feedback from you once daily, Carlos about twice as often (on average once in the morning and once every afternoon), and Jimmy once every class period (six to eight times per day). So what does this 4:1 ratio look like with these three kids in concert with all the other students in your classroom? Simply use your instincts with each student in question, coupled with your expertise and understanding about the principle of reinforcement, including your understanding of proportionality in achieving the 4:1 ratio. You know based on current levels of behavioral performance that you have a reasonably long period of time to catch the bulk of your kids in your classroom on their best behavior. In other words, their low or even nonexistent level of problem behavior grants you a larger block of time within which to provide reinforcement for expected behavior. Now in general it wouldn't hurt to reinforce the others in your classroom for prosocial behavior on a more frequent basis, but the point is that you have the luxury of more time with most of your kids based on their current levels of performance. The time interval for Jane is a bit more prescribed in that her daily rate of problem behavior (her "baseline") suggests that you may have up to no more than a full day within which to catch Jane doing things the right way on at least four occasions. Carlos, based on his needs, has a tighter time interval, in that you need to have him on your radar screen four times in the morning and four times in the afternoon, catching him doing things the correct way. Jimmy, based on his pattern of behavioral need, will require you to systematically attend to him in order to catch him doing things the correct way four times each class period in order to constructively prevent problem behavior over the longer term—and yes, for the record, Jimmy appears to be a "higher maintenance kid" than others.

This type of differentiation in your professional practice is based on student need, not preference (per se) on your part. In other words, you are not favoring one student over another; you are professionally differentiating your instructional practice based on your understanding of your students' needs. What is consistent is achieving the targeted 4:1 ratio with each of your students; what varies is the time interval within which you are working, based on the level of your students' needs.

Now of course you must be wondering, "Will the other kids who are not getting as attention as frequently as Jane, Carlos, and Jimmy rebel?" Well, it really depends on your ability to meet each of their needs for acknowledgment on an ongoing basis. Yes, those other kids will likely rebel (in various forms) if your proportionality of reinforcement does not continue to adequately address each of their needs for acknowledgment. In other words, if another kid in your classroom begins to feel like he or she is being taken for granted, then you are likely to see more frequent nuisance (and perhaps problem) behavior from him or her. This simply means you may need to shorten the time interval for reinforcement of appropriate behavior for that particular student for a brief period of time. Think back to the food analogy that I previously shared. Appropriate behavior by your other kids who have been (at least to date) behaviorally successful is likely to continue to occur as long as they feel they are being acknowledged in a manner that is meaningful. Sure, occasionally you may have one particular student who begins to voice his or her displeasure in a manner that may require you to pull that student aside for a private talk as to your expectations in this regard. As long as each of your students (in a general sense) feels as if he or she is acknowledged at a reasonable level—as viewed from his or her perspective—significant problems in this regard are unlikely to surface. The bottom line is that all your kids need reinforcement; however, not all will need reinforcement at the same exact time. The key is in achieving the 4:1 ratio with each of your students as well as with your class as a whole.

> Appropriate behavior by your other kids who have been behaviorally successful is likely to continue as long as they feel they are being acknowledged in a manner that is meaningful.

This notion of the 4:1 ratio, by the way, is not an arbitrary number or concept. It is based on practical experiences and a logical extension of the literature in terms of what has been proven to be effective. Specifically, the 4:1 ratio reflects the similar notion of proportionality as the 80%–20% split of prevention to intervention. To help you put into practice this idea of proportionality, I have provided in the Appendix descriptions of simple self-monitoring procedures relevant to achieving this 4:1 ratio in your classroom. I encourage you to consider using one of these (or another similar approach) to periodically self-monitor your reinforcement practices within your classroom.

Now, given that you have a working sense of the importance (and power) of reinforcement, it is important to select appropriate reinforcers to use with your students. Earlier I noted that what any one particular student will find reinforcing is going to be relative to him or her (e.g., public verses private praise). Therefore, you may find it helpful to identify additional things (besides your attention) that your students find desirable. You may be able to pull from information already collected about things that students find reinforcing if you happen to be teaching in a school implementing PBIS, or you may need to gather this type of information on your own. You can then utilize this information in the process of providing positive reinforcement to your students for desired behavior. There are many different ways to approach identifying potential reinforcers for use in your classroom. The most important thing to understand is that there is no preordained set of universal reinforcers—in other words, no one size fits all. Remember, what works with one student may not work with another. Also, it can be helpful to vary the reinforcers that you use to capitalize on the novelty effect—as the old adage goes, "variety is the spice of life." Table 6.2 provides four commonly used approaches to identify reinforcers for use with particular students in your classroom.

In the previous three chapters, we have looked at prevention strategies to 1) build rapport, 2) establish

Table 6.2. Common approaches to identifying reinforcers

Strategy	Description
Watch and learn	Start by observing your students during situations in which they have freedom of choice in activities and with whom they interact. In other words, to paraphrase Yogi Berra, you can see a lot by looking. Gain a sense of the things (stimuli) that your kids find enjoyable based on the choices that they exercise during situations such as free time, recess, and other nonacademic settings and routines.
Reinforcer inventory	Create a list of potential reinforcers in the format of a checklist and/or questionnaire. Use a Likert-type scale (e.g., 1 to 5, with 1 being *least desired* and 5 being *most desired*) when developing the inventory. Then have your students independently complete the inventory and review the results to gain insight into what they report. Remember that what is reported on an inventory is not always consistent with what that person may actually do in real-life situations. Therefore, some of your students may simply respond by reporting things that they think you want them to say in terms of their respective responses.
Interview students	Sit down and talk with your students (or their parents) in groups and/or one to one. Ask them about the types of things that make them feel good and/or proud, as well as the types of things that would represent their worst nightmare (in terms of the classroom). As with inventories, remember that verbal self-report (e.g. written self-report) is not as reliable or accurate a measure as actually seeing what someone does (remember the old proverb "Do as I say and not as I do").
Best guess, trial and error	Think about the ages and cultural backgrounds of your students. Specifically, what types of things are other students of similar age and backgrounds into in terms of activities of choice? Try some of these in the classroom (combine with "watch and learn"), and use the process of elimination to identify the most powerful reinforcers that you can use on a menu of options.

behavioral expectations, and 3) enhance student behavioral performance through positive reinforcement. I would urge you to view each of these three aspects of classroom management as linked with the other two components. Although each of these principles of practice is important in its own right, each is strengthened when implemented in concert with its counterparts. Much like a three-legged stool, in which no one leg balancing by itself can match the degree of strength and stability it contributes to the whole assembled piece of furniture, these components of classroom management are each rendered more effective when used together. This system of prevention can help you establish an environment conducive to learning and subsequently a welcoming classroom climate for everyone. So, although each of these three principles by themselves are of value to you as a teacher, it is in viewing these practices collectively that you can best nurture a culture of behavioral competence with your students and—to revisit the perspective of Haim Ginott (1972)—create fair weather for learning within your classroom. The whole is worth more than the sum of its parts, as the interactive effect among these principles of practice can help you establish a classroom climate conducive for learning.

> Much like a three-legged stool, in which no one leg balancing by itself can match the degree of strength and stability it contributes to the whole assembled piece of furniture, these components of classroom management are each rendered more effective when used together.

So Does It Really Boil Down to Classroom Climate?

Does classroom management really boil down to classroom climate? In a word, yes. How is that for brevity—that is, if we agree that classroom climate is a reflection of our classroom's culture as it relates to the shared belief systems, behavioral norms, and rituals that are present daily? Look, make no mistake about it: Terms such as *learning environment, learning atmosphere, classroom ecology,* and *educational milieu* are used in the field to talk with one another about our perceptions of the nature of our classrooms (i.e., classroom climate). Perceptions are funny things to understand, however. Perception is a highly personalized experience and, in many ways, much like opinion because our perceptions can become our reality. This is not necessarily a good or bad thing. It just is and therefore is something to be aware of, as our perceptions do affect how we think and act daily (including how each of us acts in the classroom). This is one of the reasons it is helpful to inform our opinions (and thus influence our perceptions) with information (e.g., our anecdotal notes as well as more formal data including discipline referrals) from which we can identify patterns and draw insight into the situations we encounter. You will likely find, however, that an overreliance on formal information (systematic data) as a prerequisite to forming opinions can freeze you like a deer in the headlights of a fast-approaching car. Suffice it to say, when it comes to classroom management, I am a firm believer in the value of *both* your gut impressions of your classroom climate and the use of a reasonable amount of formal data.

It is important and necessary to collect some data to inform your perception of classroom climate and meet the requirements of various national and state professional standards of practice. Having said this, I want to be very clear that I highly discourage blind worship at the proverbial altar of science for its own sake in the form of data collection, especially in this era of high-stakes testing in which we are increasingly compelled to collect data for (what at least on occasion appears as) data's sake.

A brief encounter that I had with a good friend and colleague of mine some time ago has stuck with me to this day. I think, in his own gentle way, he was trying to remind me that although scientific data are both useful and important, they are woefully inadequate on their own to really capture the essence of the human experience. One day, in preparation for an in-service training, we were talking about the use of data in making instructional decisions, and during a lull in the discussion, he asked me how my recent summer vacation was with my family. After I related my experience about our family trip to the shore, he asked me if I had any pictures, which would not have seemed odd if he hadn't known me well enough to know that I am not a big picture taker. In response, I said, "No. Well, a couple, but nothing that really captures the nature of the trip," to which he said, "How do you know? I mean, how do you know if you had a good time if you don't have any pictures—that is to say that you have no hard data—to support your claim? What you really have shared with me is simply your perspective with no substantiation as to how you reached that conclusion." I replied (and please remember that I knew this colleague very well, and I am giving you the *G*-rated version here for public consumption), "Wise guy, I hate it when you prove me wrong!" Now I share this not to negate the value of data (in this example, pictures

> An overreliance on formal information (systematic data) as a prerequisite to forming opinions can freeze you like a deer in the headlights of a fast-approaching car.

or other forms of keepsakes from our trip). Rather, my point is that your gut impressions, more times than not, do capture the essence of your personal experiences, whether it be your perspective of your family vacation or the climate in your classroom.

Having noted this caution, I am a proponent of collecting and using data. After all, I am a part of the academic community and to say anything to the contrary may be viewed as heresy!

A teacher's collection and analysis of data can be valuable in the classroom, especially when it comes to designing, implementing, and evaluating the impact of targeted-group as well as student-centered interventions and supports such as the type I discuss in later chapters. For example, collecting data in the form of monitoring your use of reinforcement procedures for appropriate student behavior as compared with your use of redirection procedures in response to student problem behavior can be invaluable. You are encouraged to focus on your data collection on a periodic basis focusing on two aspects of behavioral performance (or units of analysis): 1) your class of students as a whole, in aggregate, and 2) specific students who appear at risk for developing serious problem behavior. A data collection sheet that you can use in your tabulation efforts both to self-monitor your achievement of the 4:1 ratio as well as to document the frequency of student problem behavior is in the Appendix and online. This resource can be used to track individual student performance (in connection to your reinforcement and redirection procedures) as well as student performance in aggregate. You are encouraged to use this approach on a scheduled basis to gain a periodic snapshot of your classroom.

Having said this, though, both we and our students will naturally develop perceptions (a gut sense) as to the nature of the learning environment that we establish within our classroom. We can significantly influence our classroom climate and therefore the subsequent gut impressions of our students (and ourselves) as a result of implementing the three primary aspects of preventative classroom management—rapport, expectations, and positive reinforcement. In other words, the proof will be in the taste of the pudding; we will not have to wait for the pictures (or test scores) to come back to determine the learning climate of our classroom.

In a related manner, in corporate America (specifically the area of organizational management), a direct, positive correlation between worker morale and productivity has been well documented. This is, of course, related to the employees' perspectives (their gut sense, so to speak) that they will do better

> We can significantly influence our classroom climate and therefore the subsequent gut impressions of our students (and ourselves) as a result of implementing the three primary aspects of preventative classroom management—rapport, expectations, and positive reinforcement.

work if they are working in environments that are conducive to meeting their needs as well as meeting the bottom line for their employer. Likewise, as teachers, we can anticipate higher levels of student academic and behavioral success when our students feel they are working in environments that are conducive to meeting their needs as well as meeting the bottom line, which is measured by many indicators of student achievement. Specifically, educational research in tandem with everyday teaching experiences suggests more than a casual relationship among classroom climate, student morale, and achievement. Furthermore, the issue of classroom climate has been linked with teacher morale and has shown similar effects as noted in corporate America with respect to teacher satisfaction and burnout. This should not come as a surprise when we consider that all members of the classroom community have a vested interest—a shared stake, so to speak—in the feel of the classroom. Given this, each member of the classroom (each student and each teacher) in his or her own way makes a contribution to the classroom's climate. The contribution by you as the teacher goes beyond your natural role as the classroom leader and includes you as a part of the learning community with your classroom. Simply stated, the more your students are well behaved,

> As teachers, we can anticipate higher levels of student academic and behavioral achievement when our students feel they are working in environments that are conducive to meeting their needs as well as meeting the bottom line, which is measured by many indicators of student achievement.

the happier you will be. In turn, the happier you are, the happier and more successful your students will likely be both now and in the future. This, of course, increases everyone's degree of personal satisfaction, which is a good thing in any classroom.

Personal satisfaction that is based on an understanding that each person makes an important contribution to the learning climate can help further build a sense of community and resiliency both in your students as well as for you as the professional leader in your classroom. You are clearly at an advantage in this sense if you happen to be teaching in a school that is implementing PBIS with fidelity, in that collaborative decision-making structures that are organized around acknowledgment systems and forms of increasing degrees of layered preventative approaches across the entire school are likely already in place—which simply means that you have a framework within which you are already working that helps build a sense of community and resiliency across the entire school. Building resiliency is also equally important and certainly achievable in more traditional school settings. However, if you are a classroom teacher in a more traditional school setting your influence on the learning climate may be more time intensive as well as somewhat limited to your immediate classroom.

Establishing a healthy classroom climate not only involves building rapport, establishing clear expectations, and delivering positive reinforcement but also requires time-efficient ways in which to redirect students' inappropriate behavior when it surfaces. Some degree of inappropriate behavior is likely to occur on occasion within any given classroom—even a classroom such as yours despite your efforts to emphasize preventative approaches. Remember in previous chapters I described the 80% prevention–20% intervention balance of investment on your part as a teacher in managing behavior in your classroom? It can become a slippery slope in practice when we struggle to find this balance. Sometimes when we find ourselves confronted with increasing numbers of students who appear in need of greater degrees of individualization or increasing frequency of disruptive behavior we can be inadvertently drawn away from focusing on this 80%–20% balance. In other words, we may lose our way by looking for ways in which to "ramp up" our reactive (redirective) approaches and lose sight of the fact that the solution set lies in further ramping up our preventative approaches. This is not to suggest that it is not important to have clear, concise, and time-efficient procedures for redirecting students who engage in inappropriate behavior. To the contrary, this is essential to both establish and maintain a healthy learning climate. However, the key is in finding ways to further build in preventative approaches while consistently employing straightforward, routine procedures to redirect inappropriate student behavior in a manner that 1) de-escalates the situation in a time-efficient manner and 2) successfully protects instructional time on academic tasks and our rapport with our students.

For example, remember Jimmy from Chapter 6? Arguably, Jimmy creates a challenge with which any classroom teacher can identify. It is important in such a situation as presented by Jimmy's example to engage in efforts to ramp up preventative measures in tandem with implementing simple, time-efficient redirection procedures. In our next chapter we will look at two simple, time-efficient (Tier 1 level) procedures to redirect inappropriate behavior that you should find useful within your classroom. These procedures should prove helpful to you in redirecting inappropriate behavior in a manner that can best position you to achieve the 80% prevention–20% intervention balance in your classroom that you are striving to achieve. Furthermore, in a worst-case scenario, use of these two procedures in tandem with preventative approaches will also set the stage for more targeted group (Tier 2) or individual intensive (Tier 3) approaches should such a need emerge as a result of a given student not sufficiently responding to your good faith efforts in implementing universal prevention (Tier 1) procedures within your classroom.

So How Do I Address Inappropriate Behavior?

Understandably, you must be thinking, "When and how do I intervene with Jimmy and any other student who does not seem to be sufficiently responding to my preventative approach to classroom management?" Well, for starters, don't panic. You should find that the preventative approaches that we have focused on should work sufficiently well with most of your students. However, there will likely be a given student along the way who will require more intervention and support than other students in your classroom.

Let me reiterate a point that I described for consideration in Chapter 3 with respect to responding to inappropriate student behavior. It is important to differentiate between nuisance behavior and problem behavior, as each warrants a different type of response. As the old saying goes, you do not want to make a mountain out of a molehill (i.e., overreact to nuisance-level behavior). But you also do not want minor waves in your classroom pool to become tsunamis (i.e., nuisance behavior escalating into significant problem behavior). Furthermore, it is important to remember that how you respond to both nuisance and problem behavior will take place within the context of your overall approach to classroom management (i.e., the preventative principles of practice we have been looking at thus far). Along these same lines, as teachers we are always teaching through our actions, which includes modeling how to respond to others who are acting inappropriately. Remember, your students are always watching you.

As a reminder, nuisance behaviors are the things that kids do that alone are inconsequential. In other words, if you pulled the actual inappropriate behavior out of context to look at it in isolation (as in a vacuum or under the proverbial microscope so to speak) the actual inappropriate behavior would likely not look like a big deal. However, such nuisance behaviors can really wear you down over time in the classroom. For example, frequent minor occurrences of off-task behavior with a particular student or group of students can really get on your nerves—thus the importance of teacher self-management of instructional practice when in group settings. Nuisance (inconsequential) behavior is best addressed through indirect intervention—thus, not calling attention to the student while he or she is engaged in the nuisance behavior (or "junk" behavior [Latham, 1999]). There are generally two contexts in which you may need to systematically ignore nuisance behavior. In one-to-one situations you can simply not respond to Jimmy's nuisance behavior. Rather, focus on things that he is doing correctly and avoid feeding your visible attention into his inappropriate behavior (e.g., fidgeting, perseverations, and brief moments of off-task behavior). During group instructional situations, when Jimmy engages in inappropriate behavior simply find other students who are engaged in appropriate behavior who are in close physical proximity to Jimmy. Keep Jimmy on your radar screen in a way that does not suggest to Jimmy that you are watching him (in other words, you are watching him without him realizing that you are watching him). Reinforce those other students one at a time for appropriate behavior and do not respond to Jimmy's nuisance behavior. Next, explicitly reinforce Jimmy for appropriate behavior once he ceases the nuisance behavior and engages in desired behavior (e.g., on-task behavior). In both of these situations, the key strategy is that you want to ignore the student's nuisance behavior rather than feeding into it. Use the same reinforcement procedures that were described in Chapter 6 for appropriate behavior. Using this approach to indirectly respond to inconsequential behavior should help position you to act in a manner consistent with the preventative approaches that have been previously highlighted (i.e., achieving the 80%-20% balance).

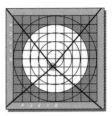

Inappropriate behavior ceases to be inconsequential when the behavior of concern persists for an unacceptable amount of time (e.g., Jimmy being off task for longer than you view as reasonable despite your efforts to indirectly intervene as described previously) or when the behavior of concern becomes disruptive or potentially harmful (e.g., pulling other kids off task or creating an unsafe situation). When problem behavior occurs, you should directly intervene employing a basic three-step process: 1) tell the student (e.g., Jimmy) to stop the problem behavior (e.g., name-calling, being out of his seat, interrupting classmates), 2) direct Jimmy to perform an appropriate behavior, and 3) reinforce Jimmy once he complies with your redirection. To be clear, you are not reinforcing Jimmy for the problem behavior. Rather, you are reinforcing Jimmy for compliance with your redirection when he performs the alternative appropriate behavior

> Nuisance (inconsequential) behavior is best addressed through indirect intervention.

(be sure to be explicit about what you are reinforcing by labeling your praise). When using a direct intervention procedure, keep your words and actions to a minimum, thus allowing you to be time efficient while observing how the student (Jimmy in this situation) responds. Furthermore, keeping your words and actions to a minimum reduces the likelihood of getting drawn into long conversations (at least at this point in time) and will also make you less susceptible to what is referred to as "bait and switch" tactics at which some students become masterful (e.g., the student placing blame elsewhere, making accusations of being picked on or singled out by you, or saying other things that enable the student to switch your focus from the particular student's behavior to tangentially related issues). You are also encouraged to provide corrective feedback (when needed) in as private a manner as feasible to minimize the likelihood of public power struggles (helping the student and you "save face"). Table 8.1 outlines a basic three-part script that I encourage you to consider when using direct intervention procedures.

> When using a direct intervention procedure, keep your words and actions to a minimum, thus allowing you to be time efficient while observing how the student responds.

The key in using redirection procedures efficiently is in having their use become habitual to you within the ebb and flow of your daily activities in your classroom. As I stated before, we all develop habits; the key is in developing effective habits of practice. As such, the goal for you is to move beyond the initial acquisition phase (in which thinking and walking through the procedures is a cognitive task) to the point at which your use of these redirection

Table 8.1. Three-part script to redirect a given student's problem behavior

Step in process	What to say
Part 1 In the instance in which Jimmy engages in problem behavior, you want to directly intervene by getting in close physical proximity and assertively stopping him from continuing in the problem behavior.	Represent the problem behavior, be specific, and label the problem behavior (e.g., "Jimmy, stop grabbing John's materials off his desk").
Part 2 Once you have gained Jimmy's attention with your "stop" statement, you will redirect Jimmy to an alternative behavior that is in keeping with your expectations.	Represent the alternative behavior (e.g., "Keep your hands on your own materials and start doing your work").
Part 3 Once you have redirected Jimmy, you will pause and wait for him to respond. If Jimmy does not comply, then simply repeat your verbal redirection, adding additional prompts and cues to enable student compliance. Once compliance occurs, provide reinforcement for following your redirection.	Provide explicit verbal praise for compliance (e.g., "Thank you, Jimmy, for using your own materials and doing your work").

procedures becomes associative in nature (meaning that you can implement the procedures without losing focus on the rest of your class). There is no shortcut from acquisition to fluency in use of these procedures…or at least none of which I am aware. As such, the key becomes preparation through practice (ideally through simulation activities with your colleagues) and then, of course, consistent application in your classroom. Although practice doesn't always make perfect when it comes to real-life situations, practice can help you be more prepared for those real-life situations. So do yourself a favor and practice, practice, practice. Over time use of these procedures can become almost rote in nature and help you be more effective (and time efficient) in redirecting inappropriate student behavior. Having your use of these procedures become routine in nature can be particularly helpful in the event that a given student engages in particular forms of misbehavior that are personally aggravating to you (your personal triggers, so to speak) as well as in the event that you are not feeling particularly resilient on a given day (e.g., working through having a cold and/or feeling run down).

> 1) Acknowledging appropriate behavior in the form of praise is a relatively cost-effective form of reinforcement that you can easily use daily in your classroom and 2) fairness really means that everyone gets what he or she needs with the understanding that needs will vary from student to student and that these needs change over time and across situations.

The need to redirect inappropriate student behavior is inevitable in any classroom. This will be the case for you in your classroom regardless of whether you are teaching in a school implementing PBIS with fidelity or a more traditional school setting. Therefore, becoming fluent in both indirect and direct intervention should prove valuable to you in your classroom. Remember that your primary (if not sole) objective at the moment of indirect or direct intervention is to simply redirect the student of concern (such as Jimmy) to engage in appropriate (desired) behavior. Sometimes, on the rare occasion that we lose perspective and our ability to self-manage our instructional practice at a moment in time, we can get sucked into situations that can result in teaching performance that is counterproductive (e.g., overreacting to nuisance behavior or harshly redirecting a student). It is important to keep a clear eye on the intended outcome of your use of a redirection procedure as previously described. A good way to think about this is through analogy. To illustrate, imagine that the fire department (with trucks and fire fighters) arrived at a building that was ablaze and their initial actions were to stand around and talk about 1) how the fire started and 2) how to prevent fires in this building in the future. This, of course, makes no sense, as the primary task at hand is to put out the fire to minimize damage. This is not to suggest that having a discussion about the origin of the fire and how to prevent reoccurrence in  the future is not a good idea, as that conversation could prove very helpful, but it should occur later on in time. The primary task is to stop the fire in its tracks to minimize spread and damage. This is precisely the same way redirection procedures in the classroom operate. Your primary (if not sole) objective when redirecting a given student is to get the "fire" to stop by redirecting the student to a more desired course of action (behavior) at that moment in time. Keeping this clearly in mind can help you more effectively self-manage your instructional practice when the need arises to redirect a student for inappropriate behavior.

Now having described these two general redirection procedures, it is important to remember that you may still encounter a given student (or two) with whom you find yourself needing to use redirection procedures more frequently than desired. This does *not* mean that your redirection procedures are not working; on the contrary, the fact that the student of concern complies with a redirection procedures indicates that the procedure had the immediate desired effect. Rather, what can happen on occasion is that a given student's needs may require more than

> Your primary objective when redirecting a given student is to get the "fire" to stop by redirecting the student to a more desired course of action (behavior) at that moment in time.

the array of preventative Tier 1 (universal level) procedures described thus far. In such situations it is important to consider integrating Tier 2 (targeted group level) strategies by building on (or layering on top of) Tier 1 approaches. To be clear, addressing the needs of a student who is not sufficiently responding to your Tier 1, preventative approaches does *not* entail aborting your universal preventative approaches. Rather, much like adding on additional layers of clothing when you are cold, you will need to strategically layer Tier 2 approaches on top of Tier 1 practices, as I will describe in the next chapter.

So What Else Can I Do?

Now if you find yourself increasingly using redirection procedures as just described with a student in your classroom, such as Jimmy, despite your good faith efforts to increase your use of preventative procedures, you are likely struggling to achieve the 4:1 ratio of reinforcement to corrective feedback that was described in Chapter 6. Another way to state this is that the student of concern is not sufficiently responding to your Tier 1 (universal level) approaches in your classroom and therefore you have need to layer on top of your Tier 1 procedures Tier 2 (targeted group level) approaches. This approach to problem solving (i.e., layer on additional Tier 2 supports) is both logical and relevant for you whether you are teaching in a PBIS school or a more traditional school setting.

One of the hallmarks of Tier 2 approaches is the increased use of progress monitoring in tandem with establishing procedures to modify interventions and supports as needed with the student of concern. It is important that any form of strategies as well as modifications that you implement have clearly defined features that also include provisions for the gradual decrease (or tapering) of targeted interventions and supports as your student experiences increasing degrees of improved behavior over time.

Increased frequency of progress monitoring including data collection and analysis is an essential aspect of Tier 2 approaches. Your progress-monitoring procedures should dovetail efficiently with your approach to preventative classroom management as described in previous chapters. In other words, implementation of the Tier 1 approaches previously outlined should position you to "work smarter" as you layer on Tier 2 procedures.

In addition to increased (more systematic) progress monitoring, an additional hallmark of Tier 2 approaches is reclarification, reteaching, and increased positive reinforcement of the student for meeting the performance expectations that you have already established within your classroom. To be blunt, you are not looking to alter (or dumb down, so to speak) the behavioral expectations in your classroom. In fact, those expectations serve as a form of a social skills curriculum within your classroom. Rather, Tier 2 approaches are simply targeted interventions and supports that provide increasingly precise (and systematic) instructional practices to support student achievement of those same behavioral competencies that you have already established in your classroom (e.g., be here, be ready, be responsible, be respectful).

There are two important factors to take into account as you begin to plan targeted interventions and supports with your student of concern. First, it is important to understand that there are a variety (or a menu of options) of Tier 2 interventions and supports to consider. Second, the context within which you are teaching will likely influence which Tier 2 approaches will make the most sense for you to implement (finding the right match, sometimes referred to as contextual fit, is important to meeting everyone's needs within your classroom). Specifically, you will likely have at your disposal a broad array of Tier 2 options from which to select if you are teaching within a PBIS school. However, there are options (even though fewer and perhaps more cumbersome for you as a classroom teacher to employ) if you are teaching within a more traditional school system that may not have formally established MTSS (in the form of PBIS). In light of the importance of finding the right match of Tier 2 approaches for your classroom, I have provided you with some guidance that highlights implementation of Tier 2 approaches in PBIS schools as well as more traditional school programs.

> Implementation of the Tier 1 approaches previously outlined should position you to "work smarter" as you layer on Tier 2 approaches.

TIER 2 APPROACHES WITHIN POSITIVE BEHAVIORAL INTERVENTIONS AND SUPPORTS SCHOOLS

One valuable resource that you can build on is the established data collection system that should already be in place if you are working within a PBIS school (e.g., SWIS). Specifically, utilizing SWIS in analyzing the data patterns that may exist within your classroom can be very helpful in organizing early identification of students who appear in need of Tier 2 supportive interventions. To be most effective, students must be able to quickly access Tier 2 level practices in a timely manner when needed. Given this, it should be helpful to draw from preexistent data to facilitate early identification and intervention. Beyond the obvious use of discipline referrals, other examples of existent data sources that can be reviewed include attendance, tardiness records, completion of credit hours toward graduation, and performance on high-stakes testing required for graduation at the secondary level as well as work/course completion including grades across all grade levels.

One example of a targeted approach that is commonly available in PBIS schools is known as Check & Connect

(Sinclair et al., 1998). In Check & Connect an identified staff member (usually *not* a given student's classroom teacher) serves as a primary point of contact and reference for the student of concern. This person may perform many important duties, which typically includes meeting with the student of concern on a periodic basis. In addition, this person may serve as a liaison among relevant people, including the student and members of his or her family as well as staff at school and people who may be able to provide natural support in the local community. PBIS schools implementing Check & Connect typically establish two levels of operations within this approach (often referred to as "basic" and "intensive"). The basic level features the assigned staff member meeting with the student on a less frequent basis (e.g., perhaps once a month) as compared with more frequent meetings and interactions at the intensive level. Meetings typically focus on progress updates on school performance and applying problem-solving approaches. Direct review and reteaching of social skills is commonly a part of this approach in PBIS schools. So logically you will want to speak with your PBIS leadership team (or start with your school administrator) to be sure that you can access this Tier 2 approach if your school has established this as one of your Tier 2 programs. I have provided some references on Check & Connect, which can be particularly helpful in improving performance by students whose inappropriate behavior appears to be attention motivated, for your convenience.

Another Tier 2 approach that is typically on the menu of options in PBIS schools is the Behavior Education Program (Crone et al., 2004). This program is also referred to in many schools as Check-In: Check-Out (CICO), which can be particularly helpful in improving the performance of students whose inappropriate behavior appears escape motivated. One similarity to the Check & Connect approach is that CICO emphasizes scheduled meetings with the student of concern. However, CICO is organized around scheduled daily meetings. Most schools implementing CICO identify a common staff member (often a paraprofessional) with whom the targeted students check in at the start of the school day and check out at the end of the day (or in some instances a.m. and p.m. check-in and check-out). Check-in meetings usually focus on preparedness for the school day (e.g., homework, materials, and a daily progress report [DPR] that, in most cases, the student presents to his or her teachers upon entry to each classroom throughout the day). Check-out meetings mostly focus on tallying the daily points earned by the given student (keeping in mind that the DPRs focus on the schoolwide expectations that are already established) in concert with the delivery of additional acknowledgment for performance, guidance, and encouragement. Furthermore, many PBIS schools build a home communication element into their implementation of CICO, in which the student brings the DPR home for review (and in many instances parent signature). As with Check & Connect, you are encouraged to access this form of Tier 2 supportive intervention if it is provided on your school's menu of options for targeted interventions and supports. I have, as well, provided you with some references for CICO in the References and Resources for Further Reading for your convenience.

Some PBIS schools actually provide both Check & Connect and CICO at Tier 2 to support their students. In such instances, Check & Connect (basic level) is usually the initial form of Tier 2 support provided with CICO reserved for timely access if or when the student of concern does not sufficiently respond to Check & Connect. This is both logical and consistent with the organizational framework that drives MTSS in the form of PBIS. In either case, whether both or only one option is on your menu of options in your school, you will want to access these additional organized supports for you and your students when needed.

An additional approach that is commonly a part of Tier 2 approaches in PBIS schools is the incorporation of targeted social skills training. In many instances students are scheduled for reteaching activities associated with the schoolwide expectations. This is not to suggest that social skills instruction is not occurring as a part of Tier 1 endeavors across the school (e.g., such as within the ebb and flow of a typical day in your classroom). Rather, as a Tier 2 strategy, this provides a way to bring those students who appear to need additional instruction and feedback in social skills together to provide additional instruction. Usually this reteaching occurs in small group settings. Schools tend to go about organizing the reteaching sessions in a variety of ways. As such, this means that you may (or may not) have direct involvement in delivering these additional small group remedial sessions. However, at a minimum as the classroom teacher, you should be in the loop of information and providing guidance and feedback on an ongoing basis to the student of concern in your classroom.

Mentoring represents yet another Tier 2 approach that has been implemented in school systems with success. Again, as with the previously described Tier 2 approaches, the foundation of mentoring is in fostering connectedness within the school (and the community in an extended sense). Mentoring, in a somewhat unique manner, often tends to further foster varying forms of more naturally occurring support systems for students in both the school and community. This, of course, is somewhat dependent on how the mentoring program is designed. In my experiences, rarely should a mentoring program serve as the only Tier 2 approach in a PBIS school. However, mentoring programs are often incorporated as a part of an array of Tier 2 approaches (e.g., mentoring in tandem with Check & Connect and/or CICO). Schools that have employed mentoring approaches have either worked with existent mentoring initiatives (e.g., Big Brothers and Big Sisters) or established their own mechanisms through collaboration with local community resources. As with the previous Tier 2 approaches described, as a classroom teacher in a PBIS school you will want to make sure you are aware and connected with mentoring options that your school provides at Tier 2.

What is very evident about the described Tier 2 approaches in a PBIS school is that you, as the teacher trying to effectively work with a student who is not sufficiently responding to your Tier 1 approaches, are not working in isolation with the student of concern. Check & Connect, CICO, targeted social skills instruction, and mentoring programs are collaborative endeavors commonly present on the Tier 2 menu of options within a PBIS school. In other words, you are *not* alone when trying to layer on Tier 2 approaches with a particular student in your classroom within a PBIS school.

TIER 2 APPROACHES
WITHIN TRADITIONAL SCHOOLS

If you teach in a traditional school setting, although you may not have access to the benefits associated with PBIS data systems or the array of collaborative options of Tier 2 approaches commonly available in PBIS schools, all is not lost! You will likely base the identification of students in your classroom who appear in need of targeted intervention and support on your intuitive sense for how your students are responding to your approach to classroom management. Although obviously your use of intuition may not be as reliable as documented discipline referrals, use of your intuitive sense may serve as your most accessible form of information to inform your practice in your classroom (at least to start). The bottom line is that as a teacher you can only use what you have access to at that moment in time, so use to the best of your ability the information that is available. By way of these comments I am not suggesting that it is not possible to have an array of targeted interventions and supports available at your school building. My experience suggests that most traditional schools have, in their own way, at least some array of options. In fact many schools have an array of well-intended initiatives in place. Unfortunately, without proper organization such initiatives, despite good intent and resources, commonly can appear disjointed and difficult to access. Often frontline folks, such as you as the classroom teacher, are left to try to navigate the array of available resources without a clear and explicit protocol that is organized into a multitiered framework. Furthermore, often the focal point of Tier 2 strategies in more traditional schools tends to reflect you as the classroom teacher taking on more and more responsibility in isolation to address your particular student of concern's needs, which may require Herculean efforts on your part (and thus may not be sustainable over time). To be clear, I am not suggesting that continued overreliance on you as the teacher taking on increasing degrees of workload is by design in most traditional schools. Rather, it simply can become the practical result (despite intentions to the contrary) when a coherent multitiered organization of intervention and supports is lacking.

One initial Tier 2 approach worth exploration in your classroom is an adaptation of the use of DPRs from the Behavior Education Program (Check-In, Check-Out [CICO]). I suggest starting with an adaptation of this approach, as it provides you, as the classroom teacher, with a form of targeted intervention that is within your direct reach (or ability to implement). In other words, should you find yourself needing to explore Tier 2 approaches devoid of a formal MTSS at your school, adaption of DPRs may prove to be a reasonably efficient place to start. To help keep things clear and to distinguish DPRs associated with CICO from the adapted application I

You are *not* alone when trying to layer on Tier 2 approaches with a particular student in your classroom within a PBIS school.

am suggesting, I will refer to this adapted approach as behavior progress reports (BPRs). For your convenience, reproducible BPRs are in the Appendix and online. You will need to target what you believe to be a reasonable time interval for use of this adapted approach. DPRs associated with CICO (as indicated in the name) reflect the student's behavior based on a daily time frame. However, there are typically multiple measures that occur with CICO within a given school day as the student goes from class to class between the check-in and check-out sessions (e.g., three measures in the morning and three in the afternoon, plus the lunch period, resulting in seven measures in a given day). Of course application of CICO requires an infrastructure of coordination that comes with MTSS (e.g., PBIS), as multiple staff may be involved in the process along with the student of concern. Thus you will want to start by identifying what you feel to be a manageable time interval for measures as you apply your BPRs in your classroom with the student of concern. For example, you may want to start with fewer measures in a given day and, in turn, debrief with your student of concern on a scheduled basis that you can consistently employ (e.g., in a second-grade classroom perhaps one morning and one afternoon measure per day and meeting to review progress once or twice per week). To be clear, I am not suggesting that such an adapted approach will be as precise, effective, or efficient as systematic application of DPRs within CICO. Rather, the use of BPRs as described may provide you with a logical place to start in the event that you do not have access to additional supports to run high-fidelity CICO. Applying BPRs as described will provide you with an approach that reflects increased progress monitoring with your student of concern. You, of course, may adjust the frequency of measures and debriefing sessions as appropriate based on student progress (or lack of a sufficient rate of progress) as well as other factors in your classroom (e.g., sustainability of your data collection in tandem with interventions and supports). Also, of great importance is that you remember that you are encouraged to continue application of Tier 1 strategies as described in previous chapters in tandem with layering on your use of BPRs as needed.

In the event that your student of concern does not sufficiently respond to your use of BPRs you may need to consider a more comprehensive approach to behavior contracting with the student of concern. There are two important concepts to keep in mind when developing a behavior contract. First, the primary goal of a behavior contract is to see sufficient improvement in behavior so that you can wean the student off the contract within a reasonable amount of time. Second, at its very core, a behavior contract is nothing more than a systematic, student-centered way of further defining behavioral expectations and increasing the likelihood of being able to catch your student doing things the correct way. An effective student-centered contract should enable you to reinforce the student for desired

behavior at a more sufficient rate based on his performance. (Thus behavior contracts are consistent with the
principle of reinforcement that
I emphasized in Chapter 6.)
This is typically accomplished
by further operationally defining the same behavioral expectations that you have for all
your students while also establishing a clear criterion for
performance within a reasonable (typically shorter) time
interval for that given student.
In short, an effective behavior

> A behavior contract
> is nothing more than
> a way of defining
> behavioral expectations
> and increasing the
> likelihood of being able
> to catch students doing
> things the correct way.

contract has more to do with reinforcement procedures for
appropriate behavior than it has to do with negative consequences (given, of course, that you select meaningful
reinforcement procedures for the student in question). An
example of a behavior contract is provided in the Appendix for your review.

Beyond use of BPRs and behavior contracts, it is certainly appropriate to consider the use of some form of
mentor program as previously described with the particular student of concern. In fact, the power of noncontingent
reinforcement and attention (e.g., personal greetings)
serves as a building block in building rapport. Connecting the student with an adult of his or her preference to
provide periodic support and guidance can help reduce
problem behavior (e.g., if the mentor is available daily at
school the student could periodically touch base with his
or her mentor each day). Mentoring programs may be used
in tandem with BPRs as well as behavior contracting.

Obviously there are clear advantages to you as a
teacher to accessing existent resources at your school
to support your endeavors in applying targeted interventions and supports. Likewise, your use of evidenced-based

instructional practices that help prevent problem behavior is also part of the ebb and flow in an effective classroom (e.g., student choice of task sequence when appropriate, task variation, varying task difficulty). In my experiences PBIS schools that have schoolwide organization of MTSS tend to have greater natural capacity to support teachers in meeting the needs of students in need of Tier 2 (as well as Tier 3) approaches. In light of this reality, I highly encourage you to concurrently engage colleagues at your school in discussions about establishing MTSS (e.g., PBIS). Although there is rarely a convenient time to initiate these types of conversations during a school year, I believe it is essential to have these discussions in order to build such capacity in your school system. I have provided some guidance for your consideration for initiating such discussions with your colleagues in the Appendix.

10

So What if Everything I Have Tried Is Still Not Working? What Else Can I Do?

You are likely asking yourself where you can turn and what else you can do if all your efforts in applying Tier 1 and 2 approaches thus far have failed to yield sufficient results with your student of concern (e.g., Jimmy). Well, all is not lost by any means. In fact, all your efforts thus far with your student have set the stage for layering on Tier 3 (individual intensive) approaches.

Before going into any initial level of detail on individualized intensive interventions and supports, I need to be sure that you have a practical and realistic understanding of Tier 3 approaches—otherwise I may inadvertently set you up for additional frustration. The development and implementation of effective and sustainable student-centered, individual-intensive approaches requires a team approach. Let me reiterate this very important point: It requires a *team* approach. In my experiences, if a student truly is in need of Tier 3 behavior interventions and supports, no one classroom teacher in isolation will be able to comprehensively meet all the needs of the student of concern. A team approach is necessary when a student's needs are so pronounced as to require Tier 3 approaches. In a similar manner to that described in the prior chapter on Tier 2 approaches, in my experiences school systems that have in place well-organized MTSS in the form of PBIS tend to have an inherent capacity to layer on Tier 3 approaches in an effective and sustainable manner. However, I have also witnessed (albeit to a lesser degree) effective team-oriented behavior intervention and support in more traditional schools. There are many factors to consider when confronted with the need to organize a student-centered behavior intervention and support team whether you are working in a PBIS or more traditional school setting. So, in light of this reality, let me start by providing some guidance to you as you begin to organize a team approach to implementing individual-intensive approaches to address the needs of your student of concern. Often the term *team* can become a nasty four-letter word in schools if both the structure and process of a team collaborative approach are not thoughtfully designed and implemented. There should already be some formal structure and defined process for organizing and operating a student-centered team approach when warranted if you are teaching in a PBIS school. In this case you will want to start by familiarizing yourself with those existent structures and processes to work in the most efficient manner possible. I have provided some teaming tips in the Appendix that I would encourage be incorporated within those existent teaming structures and processes (should they not already be in place in your PBIS school). You should also find these tips on teaming useful in more traditional school settings.

There are likely, at least to some degree, also existent structures and processes in more traditional school programs to try to organize resources to address the needs of students with significant social/emotional/behavioral needs. As I commented on Tier 2 approaches in the prior chapter, despite good intent of efforts by staff, many times these structures and processes tend to appear confusing or illusive for many teachers if not organized within an MTSS framework. This can also be further compounded when the student of concern may happen to have a disability and, as a result, the governing force of teaming activities can drift toward being exclusively focused on compliance with procedural safeguards inherent within the special education process. By saying this I am not suggesting that such procedural safeguards are not relevant or important—on the contrary, they are important. However, based on my experiences, I caution that the focal point for the given team can easily become exclusively focused on matters of compliance as opposed to organizing interventions and supports in a manner that makes a positive difference in tandem with complying with special education requirements. Suffice it to say that you may find it challenging to organize an effectively functioning team within such a traditional school setting. In such situations, I encourage you to start by talking with your relevant school administrator (e.g., principal) about establishing a team approach with the student of concern. I have provided some guidance in the Appendix for your consideration should you need to organize a student-centered team. Once you have established the team, it is now ready to begin to operate.

First and foremost, it is important to keep things in perspective and to remember that one of the keys to effectively intervening and supporting your student at this next level will be to understand why he or she (in our case, Jimmy) engages in problem behavior in tandem with layering on greater degrees of specificity in matching strategies with assessment results. Decoding student behavior in this manner should prove helpful in organizing sustainable interventions and supports. A functional behavior assessment (FBA) is the process of gathering information that can help you understand the reason for

Jimmy's problem behavior. This assessment process is also the same FBA procedure that is required in the Individuals with Disabilities Education Improvement Act (IDEA) of 2004 (PL 108-446). Numerous published resources are available should you need to conduct a comprehensive FBA. I will briefly describe the basic principles in conducting an initial (entry-level, or what is sometimes called intuitive) FBA here; however, you are encouraged to seek more in-depth reference materials (some of which are noted in the References and Resources for Further Reading) should you find yourself needing to conduct a more comprehensive FBA.

For starters, it is important to remember that behavior occurs within a context. For example, Jimmy's behavior is connected to the classroom environment, and his problem behavior is not random in nature (even though it may feel as such to you and your fellow team members). Furthermore, it is equally important to understand that behavior also serves a purpose, which is referred to as its *function*, for the student engaging in the behavior of concern. For example, let's say that Jimmy disrupts the class by making loud noises, saying derogatory comments, and repeatedly being off task and out of his seat—in other words, he is a real handful. You find that you can get him back on task and settle him down with some basic redirection procedures, but this is fast becoming an interactive dance that you have with Jimmy on a frequent basis. In fact, you are increasingly concerned that if this pattern persists, Jimmy will be spending significant portions of his school day in various forms of time-out (in your room as well as in the principal's office). Where do you start, and how do you progress with Jimmy should he continue to misbehave regularly? Here is where understanding both *context and function* of a given student's problem behavior comes into play.

Although I have placed great emphasis on preventative approaches thus far, you will (of course) also need to respond to nuisance as well as problem behavior when it occurs (and with Jimmy, problem behavior most certainly is increasingly occurring). In other words, although you want to spend the majority of the time that you invest in classroom management on preventative approaches, you will also need to react to student behavioral errors. Understandably, you will respond to such situations with preplanned reactive interventions that have the intent of reducing or stopping the inappropriate behavior at that moment in time. This is both logical and the professionally responsible thing to do. As teachers, however, we often can become blinded by the intent of our interventions to such a degree that it can hinder our ability to see what is actually occurring by decoding the nature (context and function) of a given student's problem behavior. This can sometimes occur when we have found that a particular set of interventions or supports have worked well with one student but do not have the same result with another student. Let's continue with the example of Jimmy. Say that you have been redirecting Jimmy when he engages in these problem behaviors by sending him to time-out in response to his increasing outbursts with the hope that time-out would reduce the likelihood of future reoccurrence of Jimmy's name-calling, noise making, and overall off-task behavior. Despite your intent hard work, the problem behavior has actually been increasing—just the opposite of what you intended. Jimmy increasingly appears to you as "intervention resistant." In other words, he is not responding the way you want him to respond. Now here is where keeping things in perspective becomes really important. Because of his increasingly unacceptable behavior, it is predictable that you may start acting in a manner that appears less nurturing. Although certainly not by your design, this is a natural human response, as you are becoming more frustrated with Jimmy and his behavior on many levels for many reasons. It is important not to mistake continued misbehavior by a given student as a lack of motivation, as the student is likely motivated, just not in the desired direction. To paraphrase Saint Thomas Aquinas, the only difference between a great saint and great sinner is direction. What we are really trying to do through our approaches is to harness the student's motivation in a more constructive direction. When we become frustrated, we ourselves become at risk to engage in (or continue with) interventions and approaches that make little sense in terms of making the situation better. In such instances, it is important to take a step back and try to interpret exactly how Jimmy is responding to your current approach and to also try to decode patterns with respect to the occurrence as well as nonoccurrence of Jimmy's problem behavior (e.g., are there particular classes, times of the day, and/or situations in which Jimmy's behavior is better or worse?). One of the biggest hurdles for any teacher in decoding the reasons behind a given student's problem behavior is often a combination of our current reactive habits coupled with increasing degrees of frustration. In other words, our professional judgment is more likely to become clouded when we become upset at a given student's lack of response to our efforts. Given the information that I shared with you in previous chapters concerning Jimmy, it would appear that the use of time-out in response to his disruptiveness is not reducing or eliminating the likelihood of future reoccurrence of the problem behavior of concern. On the contrary, it actually appears that the use of time-out is

> Understandably, you will respond to disruptive situations with reactive interventions that have the intent of reducing or stopping the inappropriate behavior at that moment in time. This is both logical and the professionally responsible thing to do.

associated with increasing levels of disruptiveness over time. After reflecting on Jimmy's response to your interventions (including your use of time-out), it appears that Jimmy's disruptive behavior may, in fact, be motivated by the desire to escape. In other words, Jimmy becomes disruptive in order to escape the situation at hand (e.g., by being sent to the time-out area, the hallway, or the office). Furthermore, it would appear that despite your intent to reduce future reoccurrence of Jimmy's problem behavior through your use of time-out, the use of your current time-out procedures may be actually reinforcing Jimmy's disruptive behavior. In other words, your typical response in the form of time-out to Jimmy's disruptiveness appears to give him what he wants: escape from the situation and/or the task at hand.

Just as professional intuition (i.e., your gut professional judgment as described in earlier chapters) is valuable to you in terms of classroom climate, it also is integral when conducting an initial (entry-level) FBA regarding Jimmy. The FBA process involves asking yourself (and in turn discussing among members of your team) a series of questions and capturing information that is relevant to your responses in order to form an educated guess or hypothesis as to the nature of Jimmy's disruptive behavior. Decoding behavior at this initial level through such informal and intuitive means represents the simplest form of FBA. The bottom line is that if you can predict when problem behavior will occur you are in a better position to prevent it in the first place. You are then in a better position to specifically identify student-centered interventions and supports that are sustainable and that make sense for Jimmy based on your hypotheses (educated guesses) that summarize the results of this initial FBA.

Now, in this one example, it appears that the function of Jimmy's disruptive behavior was to escape and avoid the situation at hand. It is important to understand that, although this was the function of Jimmy's problem behavior, there are a variety of reasons any given student might act in a disruptive manner. Decoding the function(s) of a given student's problem behavior can help you in the classroom because it makes the selection and implementation of interventions a logical, systematic process. Minimizing the degree of random trial and error on your part by systematically creating educated guesses about the reason(s) behind Jimmy's problem behavior can help you increasingly see desired behavior change in the most time-efficient possible manner. Table 10.1 provides some examples of common consequences associated with specific functions of student problem behavior.

It is important to understand that the examples noted in Table 10.1 are just that—examples. Please do not misinterpret or overgeneralize these illustrations. In other words, determining the function of a given student's problem behavior is the result of conducting a student-centered FBA. Not all disruptive behavior by any given student will always serve the same function of escape/avoidance as was the case with Jimmy. Asking the core set of FBA questions helps you with decoding the nature of a given student's problem behavior.

> Decoding the function(s) of a given student's problem behavior can help you in the classroom because it makes the selection and implementation of interventions a logical, systematic process.

FBAs have been known to create a lot of stress for educators in the field. This has been especially well documented in instances in which a given teacher has not had the availability of an effective team structure for collaborative purposes. Compounding this sense of angst is the reality that FBAs are often written in terms of legal requirements associated with special education under IDEA 2004 or in

Table 10.1. Examples of common consequences associated with specific functions

Function	Common consequences
Escape (to avoid something) After a problem behavior occurs, the student avoids something unpleasant or terminates a situation that he or she perceives as negative. The problem behavior may serve as an escape (avoidance) function if one of these common consequences occurs.	The teacher provides assistance. The task is made easier. The student gets out of the task. Use of time-out for problem behavior increases. Performance demands are lessened. Adults stop "nagging." Peers stop teasing. The student is left alone.
To get something (access to social interaction, preferred objects or events) After a problem behavior occurs, the student gets something that he or she desires. The problem behavior may serve to get something if one of these common consequences occurs.	The student gets one-to-one teacher interaction or teacher contact increases. The teacher verbally responds (even neutral or negative comments may be desired by the student). Peers respond by laughing. Student gets more intense reactions. The student is redirected to a more enjoyable activity. The student gains access to things he or she wants (e.g., objects, activities, or other students). The student gets enjoyment or feels good as a result of engaging in the problem behavior.

professional journals that more typically look at empirical (scientific) studies with students with extreme forms of serious problem behavior. As important as it is to understand the legal requirements of conducting FBAs with students with disabilities, along with providing guidance to families and practitioners when working with students/clients with extreme forms of problem behavior, it's unfortunate that few publications emphasize more common, everyday applications of FBA procedures for classroom teachers. Given this, let me distill for you the basics of conducting an initial (entry-level) FBA.

At its very root, an FBA is nothing more than a problem-solving process that addresses a series of core questions regarding a given student and his or her problem behavior. You can gather information in many different ways when conducting an FBA. This variety of data-gathering procedures has (to some extent) added to the degree of confusion in the field about FBA. In other words, it can become difficult to see the forest (FBA) because of all the trees (potential data-collection procedures). Having said this, I have found that teams of teachers are best able to understand the assessment process by connecting the core questions associated with an FBA to other commonly used practices within their respective classrooms. For example, think about the basic approach to teaching comprehension of reading material within a classroom. Regardless of whether you are teaching young children to read for comprehension (in a general sense) or high school students to read a textbook for understanding, you look to engage your students by requiring them to think about key questions to address as they read. Guiding your students to ask the infamous five W questions—who, what, when, where, and why—when they are reading is one commonly accepted approach when teaching for comprehension, which also has relevance for your team when conducting an FBA. In essence, conducting an initial (entry-level) FBA with a given student involves asking this same series of questions with an emphasis on the student's behavior. Table 10.2 presents a series of logical W questions to ask concerning Jimmy and his disruptive behavior.

The reason for asking these questions in this sequence is to help you gain an understanding about why Jimmy engages in disruptive behavior. Insight in this regard can help you select both prevention and intervention approaches that are compatible with your approach to classroom operations and make sense to use with Jimmy. At a conceptual level, an FBA helps you to decode the series of events as

Table 10.2. Logical *W* questions

Context	Who is Jimmy with when he becomes disruptive?
	When is Jimmy's disruptive behavior most likely to occur?
	Are there particular circumstances when misbehavior is more likely?
	When is Jimmy's disruptive behavior least likely to occur?
	What is the nature of the routines and settings when Jimmy acts appropriately?
Behavior	What exactly does Jimmy do that is a problem?
	What does Jimmy look like and sound like when he is disruptive?
Consequence/ function	Why does Jimmy engage in the problem behavior? What does he get or avoid as a result of being disruptive? What is the payoff for Jimmy?

well as to decipher how each of those events relates with the others in the antecedent–behavior–consequence chain.

The FBA process helps your team to identify triggers to problem behavior in addition to helping decode the function of a given student's problem behavior. Identifying triggers in this regard can help your team identify things that you can do in a very practical sense in your classroom that should help minimize the likelihood that the student will continue to be disruptive at the same level. You logically can make changes in your classroom procedures to address identified triggers. Table 10.3 provides examples of fast and slow triggers commonly associated with problem behaviors that may be identified through an intuitive FBA process relevant to a given student's problem behavior.

Guiding your students to ask the infamous five *W* questions—who, what, when, where, and why—when they are reading is one commonly accepted approach when teaching for comprehension, which also has relevance for your team when conducting an FBA.

Table 10.3. Examples of common fast and slow triggers

General setting events (slow triggers)	Specific illness Poor diet, missed meals An upsetting experience earlier in the day Tired, poor night's sleep Limited opportunity for choice
Antecedents (fast triggers) commonly associated with escape and/or avoidance	Interruption of routines Transitions Lack of predictability Nonpreferred activity Difficult or repetitive work or task Boredom from easy work or task Too much work, overwhelmed
Antecedents (fast triggers) commonly associated with getting something (attention and/or objects and activities)	Access to a favorite object or activity is denied (often resulting in tantrums) Seeing someone else get attention Being unoccupied or unengaged Receiving low levels of attention Presence of a preferred person

Now, of course, the essential next step is to use your team's hypotheses about your student's problem behavior to identify relevant strategies to prevent problem behavior, teach socially appropriate alternative behaviors, and provide consequences that are connected to occurrence of appropriate as well as inappropriate behavior in the future. Effective student-centered behavior intervention and support plans reflect a healthy balance among these three components of prevention, teaching, and providing consequences associated with various forms of student behavior.

The development and implementation of a multicomponent support plan for an individual student is an important—and necessary—aspect of providing Tier 3 approaches. The key is using your team's hypotheses as a navigational tool in selecting interventions and supports. A basic thing to keep in mind is that the interventions and supports that are identified in a given student's behavior intervention and support plan should clearly be linked with both the triggers and function of the student's problem behavior as stated in your team's hypotheses. This, in one way, is what makes the FBA functional: It is useful to help your team design interventions and supports that help to prevent problem behavior as well as teach appropriate behavior. I have provided some guidance in the Appendix about linking your team's FBA results (hypotheses) with the selection of interventions and supports across each of these three components of a student-centered behavior intervention and support plan. In addition, I have also provided some guidance to help your team with implementation of a multicomponent support plan.

> Identifying triggers in this regard can help you identify things that you can do in a very practical sense in your classroom that should help minimize the likelihood that the student will continue to be disruptive at the same level.

So there you have it! I have divulged to you highly sensitive trade secrets that are usually reserved for those who join the secret society of proverbial "behavior experts." Consider this book the closest thing you'll get to a secret decoder ring that helps you to unlock the mysteries of student behavior. On a more serious note, I have shared some practical thinking on a continuum of responses to problem behavior organized within an MTSS framework. With that said, obviously this book does not exhaustively address all the possible situations that may arise in your classroom. Please refer to the References and Resources for Further Reading for additional references on Tier 3 approaches that emphasize FBA and student-centered behavior intervention plans.

11

So How Do I Connect the Dots?

As I noted in the opening chapter, the primary focus of this book is preventative classroom management. Given this emphasis, I have explored prevention through the three principles of practice described in earlier chapters and then progressed through a review of targeted as well as student-specific interventions and supports related to problem behavior. Furthermore, I have framed these principles of practice within the context of what has come to be described as an MTSS framework. In addition, I have provided guidance with respect to applying these preventative classroom management approaches if you are teaching within a school system that is implementing SWPBIS with fidelity or in a more traditional school setting.

Effective classroom management, regardless of the type of school you happen to be teaching in, is all about establishing a classroom climate that is conducive to learning for all your students in a manner that allows you to see (and feel) positive, tangible results from your efforts. As I noted in Chapter 7, it really does boil down to classroom climate. A classroom climate conducive for learning, however, is not something that just happens on its own. Rather, it develops over time as a result of thoughtful planning and action on your part as the classroom teacher. The key to making sense of all this is to understand that effective classroom management involves a variety of principles of practice that are employed in conjunction with one another. Also, please remember that the total (your classroom climate) becomes worth much more than simply the sum of its individual parts when the principles of 1) establishing rapport, 2) clearly defining behavioral expectations, and 3) reinforcing student performance of your behavioral expectations are proactively employed in an integrated manner. Table 11.1 provides the highlights of these three interrelated principles of preventative practice.

> A classroom climate conducive for learning is not something that just happens on its own.

Now, despite the preventative nature of these principles of practice and regardless of how thorough a job you do in implementing these preventative approaches, you will likely have a given student along the way who will require additional (layered) Tier 1, Tier 2, or Tier 3 interventions and supports. It is important to remember that responding to nuisance or problem behavior still reflects the basic tenants of preventative approaches emphasized in the early chapters of this book. When working with a student who displays varying forms of inappropriate behavior, you are encouraged to strategically increase your use of rapport-building strategies, teach and reteach your behavioral expectations, and increase your frequency of reinforcing the student for both acquisition and fluency in use of socially expected behavior in your classroom. Furthermore, you are encouraged to consider the array of targeted Tier 2 forms of interventions and supports highlighted in Chapter 9 in the instance in which student problem behavior persists despite your efforts to increase your effective use of preventative Tier 1 approaches. You are particularly encouraged to consider the information provided, as well as to explore the additional references noted in the References and Resources for Further Reading, if you need to learn more about Tier 3 approaches in the form of conducting a FBA in order to design a student-centered

Table 11.1. Three interrelated principles of preventative practice

Principle of practice	Description	Relationship to prevention
Establishing rapport	Rapport involves establishing and maintaining a trusting and caring relationship with each of your students. Rapport will naturally evolve between you and a number of your students. You will, however, have some students who appear harder to reach. It is particularly important to make a connection with these students. This is particularly the case if/when those same students who are at risk engage in undesired behavior.	The bottom line is that students will develop a higher degree of motivation to meet expectations for teachers with whom a trusting relationship has been established. Furthermore, student motivation in combination with maintaining rapport over time increases the likelihood of each of your students modeling expected behavior for their peers and best positions you to have greater opportunities to reinforce your students for meeting your expectations.
Defining behavioral expectations	Being clear about what you want your students to do helps you to establish a culture of behavioral competence within your classroom. Engage your students in defining the expectations across important settings and routines that naturally occur in your classroom. Have your students identify what they will "look like and sound like" when they are meeting your expectations.	It is essential for each of your students to be clear on what is expected, thus setting the stage for mastery (as opposed to mystery) learning. Clearly defining behavioral expectations creates the proverbial bull's-eye for which your students will aim. Having clear expectations also operationally sets the stage for you to "catch your kids being good" in terms of reinforcement procedures.

(continued)

Table 11.1. (*continued*)

Principle of practice	Description	Relationship to prevention
Reinforcing student performance	Providing each of your students with sufficient acknowledgment (in various forms) for meeting behavioral expectations is essential to prevention of problem behavior. Although you will differentiate your frequency of reinforcement among your students, strive to achieve a 4:1 ratio of positive reinforcement for performance of expected behavior as compared with corrective feedback for undesirable behavior with each of your students.	The most efficient way to build appropriate behavior with your students is through reinforcing appropriate behavior on an ongoing basis. Effective use of reinforcement procedures makes the expectations you have identified become more tangible and come to life. Furthermore, being viewed by each of your students as someone who provides positive feedback will also further solidify your level of rapport with your students on an ongoing basis.

behavior intervention and support plan. Implementation of the preventative approaches previously highlighted should help you realize success with most of your students and set the stage for time-efficient, targeted (Tier 2), and student-centered (Tier 3) behavior intervention and support. Last, but equally important, using these preventative practices should minimize the number of kids in your classroom whose behavior appears to require Tier 2 or Tier 3 level intervention and support and therefore increase your personal degree of satisfaction as a classroom teacher. After all, it is important to keep good teachers in our classrooms working with our children. Best of luck in all that you do!

> Implementation of the preventative approaches previously highlighted should help you realize success with most of your students and set the stage for time-efficient, targeted (Tier 2), and student-centered (Tier 3) behavior intervention and support.

References and Resources for Further Reading

BOOKS AND PERIODICALS

Albert, L. (1996). *Cooperative discipline.* Shoreview, MN: AGS Globe.

Alberto, P.C., & Troutman, A.C. (1999). *Applied behavior analysis for teachers* (5th ed.). Columbus, OH: Charles E. Merrill.

Anderson, A.R., Christenson, S.L., & Sinclair, M.F. (2004). Check & Connect: The importance of relationships for promoting school engagement. *Journal of School Psychology, 42,* 95–113.

Bambara, L.M., & Kern, L. (2004). *Individualized supports for students with problem behaviors: Designing positive behavior plans.* New York, NY: Guilford Press.

Bambara, L.M., & Knoster, T. (1998). *Designing positive behavior support plans.* Washington, DC: American Association on Intellectual and Developmental Disabilities.

Bambara, L.M., & Knoster, T. (2005). Designing positive behavior support plans. In M. Wehmeyer & M. Agran (Eds.), *Mental retardation and intellectual disabilities: Teaching students using innovative and research-based strategies* (pp. 149–174). Columbus, OH: Merrill/Prentice Hall.

Brooks, A., Todd, A.W., Tofflemoyer, S., & Horner, R.H. (2003). Use of functional assessment and a self-management system to increase academic engagement and work completion. *Journal of Positive Behavior Intervention, 5,* 144–152.

Bruce, A. (2002). *Building a high morale workplace.* New York, NY: McGraw-Hill.

Burke, M.D., Hagan-Burke, S., & Sugai, G. (2003). The efficacy of function-based interventions for students with learning disabilities who exhibit escape-maintained problem behavior: Preliminary results from a single case study. *Learning Disabilities Quarterly, 26,* 15–25.

Campbell, A., & Anderson, C.M. (2008). Enhancing effects of check-in/check-out with function-based support. *Behavioral Disorders, 33*(4), 233–245.

Campbell, A., & Anderson, C.M. (2011). Check-in/check-out: A systematic evaluation and component analysis. *Journal of Applied Behavior Analysis, 44*(2), 315–326.

Chafouleas, S., Riley-Tilman, T.C., & Sugai, G. (2007). *School-based behavioral assessment: Informing intervention and instruction.* New York, NY: Guilford Press.

Cheney, D., Lynass, L., Flower, A., Waugh, M., Iwaszuk, W., Mielenz, C., & Hawken, L. (2009). The check, connect, and expect program: A targeted, tier 2 intervention in the schoolwide positive behavior support model. *Preventing School Failure: Alternative Education for Children and Youth, 54*(3), 152–158. doi:10.1080/10459880903492742

Cheney, D.A., Stage, S.A., Hawken, L.S., Lynass, L., Mielenz, C., & Waugh, M. (2009). A 2-year outcome study of the check, connect, and expect intervention for students at risk for severe behavior. *Journal of Emotional and Behavioral Disorders, 17*(4), 226–243.

Christenson, S.L., Hurley, C.M., Hirsch, J.A., Kau, M., Evelo, D., & Bates, W. (1997). Check and connect: The role of monitors in supporting high-risk youth. *Reaching Today's Youth: The Community Circle of Caring Journal, 2*(1), 18–21.

Crimmins, D., Farrell, A.F., Smith, P.W., & Bailey, A. (2007). *Positive strategies for students with behavior problems.* Baltimore, MD: Paul H. Brookes Publishing Co.

Crone, D., Hawken, L., & Bergstrom, M. (2007). A demonstration of training, implementing and using functional behavioral assessment in 10 elementary and middle school settings. *Journal of Positive Behavior Interventions, 9*(1), 15–29.

Crone, D.A., & Horner, R.H. (2003). *Building positive behavior support systems in schools: Functional behavior assessment.* New York, NY: Guilford Press.

Crone, D.A., Horner, R.H., & Hawken, L. (2004). *Responding to problem behavior in schools: The Behavior Education Program.* New York, NY: Guilford Press.

Di Giulio, R.C. (2006). *Positive classroom management: A step-by-step guide to helping students succeed* (3rd ed.). Thousand Oaks, CA: Corwin Press.

Ervin, R.A., DuPaul, G.J., Kern, L., & Friman, P.C. (1998). Classroom-based functional and adjunctive assessments: Proactive approaches to intervention selection for adolescents with attention deficit hyperactivity disorder. *Journal of Applied Behavior Analysis, 31*(1), 65–78.

Evelo, D., Sinclair, M., Hurley, C., Christenson, S., & Thurlow, M. (1996). *Keeping kids in school: Using Check & Connect for dropout prevention.* Minneapolis: University of Minnesota, Institute on Community Integration.

Foster-Johnson, L., & Dunlap, G. (1993). Using functional assessment to develop effective, individualized interventions for challenging behaviors. *Teaching Exceptional Children, 25*(3), 44–50.

Freeman, R., Eber, L., Anderson, C., Irvin L., Horner, R., Bounds, M., & Dunlap, G. (2006). Building inclusive school cultures using school-wide PBS: Designing effective individual support systems for students with significant disabilities. *Research & Practice for Persons with Severe Disabilities, 31*(1), 4–17.

Gatto, J.T. (n.d.). *Underground history of American education: A schoolteacher's intimate investigation into the problem of modern schooling.* New York, NY: The Odysseus Group.

Ginott, H.G. (1972). *Teacher and child: A book for parents and teachers.* New York, NY: Macmillan.

Hawken, L. (2006). School psychologists as leaders in the implementation of a targeted intervention: The behavior education program. *School Psychology Quarterly, 21*(1), 91–111.

Hawken, L.S., MacLeod, K.S., & Rawlings, L. (2007). Effects of the behavior education program (BEP) on office discipline referrals of elementary school students. *Journal of Positive Behavior Interventions, 9*(2), 94–101.

Hoppe, S. (2004). Improving transition behavior in students with disabilities using a multimedia personal development program: Check and connect. *TechTrends: Linking Research & Practice to Improve Learning, 48*(6), 43–46.

Horner, R.H., Albin, R.W., Sprague, J.R., & Todd, A.W. (2000). Positive behavior support. In M.E. Snell & F. Brown (Eds.), *Instruction of students with severe disabilities* (5th ed., pp. 207–243). Columbus, OH: Charles E. Merrill.

Horner, R.H., & Carr, E.G. (1997). Behavioral support for students with severe disabilities: Functional assessment and comprehensive intervention. *Journal of Special Education, 31*(1), 84–104.

Individuals with Disabilities Education Improvement Act (IDEA) of 2004, PL 108-446, 20 U.S.C. §§ 1400 *et seq.*

Jackson, L., & Panyan, M.V. (2002). *Positive behavioral support in the classroom: Principles and practices.* Baltimore, MD: Paul H. Brookes Publishing Co.

Janney, R., & Snell, M.E. (2006). *Social relationships and peer support* (2nd ed.). Baltimore, MD: Paul H. Brookes Publishing Co.

Kern, L., Hilt, A.M., & Gresham, F. (2004). An evaluation of the functional behavioral assessment process used with students with or at risk for emotional and behavioral disorders. *Education & Treatment of Children, 27*(4), 440–52.

Knoster, T., & McCurdy, B. (2002). Best practices in functional behavioral assessment for designing individualized student programs. In A. Thomas & J. Grimes (Eds.), *Best practices in school psychology* (Vol. 4, pp. 1007–1028). Bethesda, MD: National Association of School Psychologists.

Latham, G.I. (1999). *Parenting with love: Making a difference in a day.* Logan, UT: P&T Ink.

Lehr, C.A., Sinclair, M.F., & Christenson, S.L. (2004). Addressing student engagement and truancy prevention during the elementary school years: A replication study of the Check & Connect model. *Journal of Education for Students Placed at Risk, 9,* 279–301.

McIntosh, K., Campbell, A.L., Russell Carter, D., & Rossetto Dickey, C. (2009). Differential effects of a two tier behavior intervention based on function of problem behavior. *Journal of Positive Behavior Interventions, 11*(2), 82–93.

Myers, D.M., Briere III, D.E., & Simonsen, B. (2010). Lessons learned from implementing a check-in/check-out behavioral program in an urban middle school. *Beyond Behavior, 19*(2), 21–27.

Newcomer, L.L., & Lewis, T.J. (2004). Functional behavioral assessment: An investigation of assessment reliability and effectiveness of function-based interventions. *Journal of Emotional and Behavioral Disorders, 12*(3), 168–181.

O'Neill, S., & Stephension, J. (2010). The use of functional behavioral assessment for students with challenging behaviors: Current patterns and experience of Australian practitioners. *Australian Journal of Educational & Developmental Psychology, 10,* 65–82.

Preciado, J., Horner, R.H., & Baker, S. (2009). Using a function-based approach to decrease problem behavior and increase academic engagement for Latino English Language Learners. *Journal of Special Education, 42*(4), 227–240.

Rosen, P. (Producer/Director). (1996/1989). *Richard Lavoie: How difficult can this be?* The F.A.T. City Workshop [Video]. Washington, DC: Public Broadcasting Service.

Simonsen, B., Myers, D., & Briere III, D. (2010). Comparing a behavioral check-in/check-out intervention to standard practice in an urban middle school using an experimental group design. *Journal of Positive Behavior Interventions, 13*(1), 31–38.

Sinclair, M.F., Christenson, S.L., Evelo, D.L., & Hurley, C.M. (1998). Dropout prevention for youth with disabilities: Efficacy of a sustained school engagement procedure. *Exceptional Children, 65*(1), 7–21.

Sinclair, M.F., Christenson, S.L., Lehr, C.A., & Anderson, A.R. (2003). Facilitating student engagement: Lessons learned from check & connect longitudinal studies. *The California School Psychologist, 8,* 29–41.

Smith, B., & Sugai, G. (2000). A self-management functional assessment-based behavior support plan for a middle school student with EBD. *Journal of Positive Behavior Interventions, 2,* 208–217.

Stage, S.A., Cheney, D., Lynass, L., Mielenz, C., & Flower, A. (2012). Three validity studies of the daily progress report in relationship to the check, connect, and expect intervention. *Journal of Positive Behavior Interventions, 14*(3), 181–191. doi:10.1177/1098300712438942

Steed, E.A. (2011). Adapting the behavior education program for preschool settings. *Beyond Behavior, 20*(1), 37–41.

Stoiber, K.C., & Gettinger, M. (2011). Functional assessment and positive support strategies for promoting resilience: Effects on teachers and high-risk children. *Psychology in Schools, 48*(7), 686–706.

Sugai, G., Horner, R.H., Dunlap, G., Hieneman, M., Lewis, T.J., Nelson, C.M.,...Ruef, M. (2000). Applying positive behavior support and functional behavioral assessment in schools. *Journal of Positive Behavior Interventions, 2*(3), 131–143.

Sundel, M., & Sundel, S.S. (2004). *Behavior change in the human services: Behavioral and cognitive principles and applications* (5th ed.). Thousand Oaks, CA: Sage Publications.

Thinkquest. (n.d.). *Discipline.* Retrieved January 28, 2008, from http://library.thinkquest.org/J002606/Discipline.html

Todd, A.W., Campbell., A.L., Meyer, G.G., & Horner, R.H. (2008). The effects of a targeted intervention to reduce problem behaviors: Elementary school implementation of check in-check out. *Journal of Positive Behavior Interventions, 10*(1), 46–55.

WEB SITES

Association for Positive Behavior Support (APBS), http://www.apbs.org

Center on Positive Behavior Intervention and Support (CPBIS) funded by the U.S. Department of Education Office of Special Education Programs (OSEP), http://www.pbis.org

Dr. Laura Riffle, http://www.behaviordoctor.org

Online Academy, University of Kansas, http://uappbs.apbs.org

Schoolwide Information System (SWIS), Educational and Community Supports of the University of Oregon, http://www.pbisapps.org

Appendix

CONTENTS

THE THREE BEES (ELEMENTARY SCHOOL)

Expectation	Arrival at school	Individual work	Teacher talking	Group activities	Changing activities
Be ready.	Go immediately to your classroom after arriving at school. Bring your homework with you to class. Be in your seat when the morning bell rings.	Have your materials open and on top of your desk. Follow directions the first time. Get to work right away.	Listen when Mrs. Lee speaks; one person speaks at a time. Write important things in your notebook.	Be focused on the group work to be completed. Have your materials with you and opened to the assigned page. Organize your group and get to work quickly (within 1 minute).	Be aware of the daily schedule. Listen for directions from Mrs. Lee. Be flexible in case the schedule changes.
Be responsible.	Be on time to school and class. Listen when Mrs. Lee speaks; one person speaks at a time. Complete your homework. Use indoor voices when speaking.	Follow directions on tests and assignments. Organize and get to work promptly. Make a good effort on all work. Speak only at appropriate times.	Think about what Mrs. Lee says. Ask Mrs. Lee questions by raising your hand. Volunteer to answer questions by raising your hand.	Focus on your work. One person speaks at a time using indoor voice. Ask for help as needed. Finish on time. Share with others while keeping your hands and feet to yourself.	Stop and put things away when Mrs. Lee says to do so. Know what materials you need for next class/activity. Keep your hands and feet to yourself. Use indoor voices when speaking.
Be respectful.	Say "hi" to friends before homeroom starts. Keep hands and feet to yourself. Listen when Mrs. Lee speaks; one person speaks at a time. Follow directions the first time.	Get to work and work quietly. Use only your materials. Ask for help by raising your hand. Make a good effort.	Listen and follow directions the first time. Think about what Mrs. Lee is saying. Ask questions by raising your hand. Volunteer to answer questions by raising your hand.	Encourage others to work cooperatively. Keep hands and feet to yourself. It is OK to disagree, but do it without being disagreeable. Be thoughtful of others.	Be thoughtful of others. Keep hands and feet to yourself. Use indoor voices. When moving in a room or hallway, always walk on the right side.

EXPECTED BEHAVIOR (MIDDLE SCHOOL)

Expectation	Start of class	Individual work	Teacher lecture	Group work	End of class
Be on time and prepared.	Arrive on time to class. Bring your notebook and writing materials. Listen when Mrs. Jones starts class (only one person speaks at a time).	Be focused on your work and ignore distractions. Remember to follow procedures for all individual assignments. Organize your work and get to work quickly after directed by Mrs. Jones.	Be focused on the current unit of instruction. Use your notebook for taking notes. Please listen and follow along when Mrs. Jones is speaking (only one person speaks at a time).	Be focused on the task to be completed. Have your notebook opened to the proper section being covered. Organize as a team quickly, and start work promptly (within 1 minute).	Adequately prepare materials to leave the classroom (e.g., place only your materials in your backpack). Leave the classroom promptly when dismissed by Mrs. Jones.
Be responsible for your actions.	Arrive on time to class. Listen when Mrs. Jones starts class (only one person speaks at a time). Come prepared by completing all assignments and readings. Follow all directions provided by Mrs. Jones as you enter the room.	Remember to follow procedures for individual work. Organize and do the best work that you can, even on a bad day. Control your actions and make your time productive.	Listen and think about points raised in Mrs. Jones's comments. Ask questions of Mrs. Jones and respond to questions. Gain attention by raising your hand; be patient.	Pay attention to your work and only your work. One person speaks at a time. Ask for help as needed. Successfully complete task within allotted time frame. Share roles on the team (e.g., recorder/time keeper).	Be sure you have written down all assignments to be completed prior to next class. Leave classroom in the same condition you found it when you arrived.

(continued)

EXPECTED BEHAVIOR (MIDDLE SCHOOL) *(continued)*

Expectation	Start of class	Individual work	Teacher lecture	Group work	End of class
Be respect-ful toward others.	Say "hello" to others using appropriate voice and language before class starts. Listen when Mrs. Jones starts class (only one person speaks at a time). Help others if asked for help.	Get to work quickly on individual work. Be on task and work quietly. Raise hand to get Mrs. Jones's attention.	Please follow along when Mrs. Jones is speaking (only one person speaks at a time). Think about what Mrs. Jones is saying.	Encourage others to be on task. Organize as a team quickly, and start work promptly (within 1 minute). Strive for consensus whenever possible.	Be patient and wait your turn if you need to speak with Mrs. Jones after class. Leave the room in an orderly manner.

PERFORMANCE EXPECTATIONS (HIGH SCHOOL)

Expectation	Start of class	During individual tests	During lecture in class	During other team activities	Outside of class time preparation
Be here/Be ready • On time • Prepared	Arrive on time to class. Bring your notebook and writing materials. Listen when Mr. Smith starts talking (only one person speaks at a time).	Be focused on the current unit tests. Remember to follow procedures for individual tests. Organize and get to work promptly.	Be focused on the current unit of instruction. Use your notebook for taking notes. Please listen and follow along when Mr. Smith is speaking (only one person speaks at a time).	Be focused on the task to be completed. Have your materials open to the proper section being covered. Organize as a team quickly, and start work promptly (within 1 minute).	Review prior class notes before next class. Adequately prepare by doing readings and assignments. Keep your materials organized.
Be responsible • Do quality work • Collaborate	Arrive on time to class. Listen when Mr. Smith starts talking (only one person speaks at a time). Come prepared by completing all assignments and readings. Follow procedures in course organizer if you miss a class.	Remember to follow procedures for individual tests. Organize and get to work promptly; make a good effort on each question. Be on task and ask for clarification as needed from Mr. Smith.	Listen and think about points raised in the lecture. Ask questions and respond to questions. Share your perspective on relevant issues to the topic at hand.	Be on task. One person speaks at a time. Ask for help as needed. Successfully complete task within allotted time frame. Share roles on the team (e.g., recorder/timekeeper).	Review prior class notes before next class. Adequately prepare by doing readings and assignments. Keep your materials organized.

(continued)

PERFORMANCE EXPECTATIONS (HIGH SCHOOL) *(continued)*

Expectation	Start of class	During individual tests	During lecture in class	During other team activities	Outside of class time preparation
Be respectful • Encourage others. • Recognize others.	Politely greet class-mates and teacher when arriving to class. Ask others how things are going. Listen when Mr. Smith starts talking (only one person speaks at a time). Provide guidance to classmates who may have been absent from last class.	Get to work quickly on individual tests. Be on task, and work quietly.	Please listen and follow along when Mr. Smith is speaking (only one person speaks at a time). Think about the concepts and practices being described; get the most you can out of the class.	Encourage others to be on task and to provide their perspective. Organize as a team quickly and start work promptly (within 1 minute). Strive for consensus wherever possible.	Review prior class notes before next class. Adequately prepare by doing readings and assignments. Keep your materials organized.

EXPECTATIONS PLANNING MATRIX

Expectations	Context 1:	Context 2:	Context 3:	Context 4:
Expectation 1:				
Expectation 2:				
Expectation 3:				
Expectation 4:				
Expectation 5:				

STRATEGIES FOR
SELF-MONITORING
THE 4:1 RATIO IN THE CLASSROOM

Strategy 1

Group: Place 20 pieces of unpopped popcorn in one pocket and 20 pieces of unpopped popcorn in another pocket at the start of the day. Remove one kernel of corn from your right pocket every time you "catch a kid being good" and provide reinforcement to that same child for meeting the behavioral expectations. Remove one kernel of corn from your left pocket every time you provide behavioral correction to one of your kids during this same day. At the end of the day, tally up how many kernels you have left in your pockets and then calculate a ratio based on your count (e.g., zero kernels remaining in your right pocket [20 delivered] vs. 15 remaining in your left pocket [5 delivered] converts to a 4:1 ratio of positive reinforcement vs. corrective feedback). You may also vary the time interval as you see appropriate (e.g., 1 hour vs. an entire day).

Individual: Replicate the group process, but focus on a given child as warranted.

Strategy 2

Group: Loosely wrap a piece of masking tape around your right wrist and your left wrist. Have a marker in your pocket. Place one slash mark on the tape around your right wrist for every time you "catch a kid being good" and provide reinforcement to that same child for meeting the behavioral expectations. Place a slash mark on your left wrist every time you provide behavioral correction to one of your kids during the same day. At the end of the day, tally how many slashes you have on your right wrist and on your left wrist and then calculate a ratio based on your count (e.g., 20 slashes on right wrist vs. five slashes on left wrist converts to a 4:1 ratio of positive reinforcement vs. corrective feedback). You may also vary the time interval as you see appropriate (e.g., 1 hour vs. an entire day).

Individual: Replicate the group process, but focus on a given child as warranted.

BEHAVIOR PROGRESS REPORT (PRIMARY CLASSROOM)

Name: _____

Date: _____

☺ = 2 points
☺ = 1 point
☹ = 0 points

Points received: _____

Points reached: _____

Daily goal reached? YES   NO

Be responsible	Early morning	Late morning	Early afternoon	Late afternoon	Daily total
Keep my hands, feet, body, and objects to myself.	☺ ☺ ☹	☺ ☺ ☹	☺ ☺ ☹	☺ ☺ ☹	☺ = __ ☺ = __ ☹ = __
Say nice things to other people.	☺ ☺ ☹	☺ ☺ ☹	☺ ☺ ☹	☺ ☺ ☹	☺ = __ ☺ = __ ☹ = __
Follow adult directions the first time.	☺ ☺ ☹	☺ ☺ ☹	☺ ☺ ☹	☺ ☺ ☹	☺ = __ ☺ = __ ☹ = __
				Grand total:	☺ = __ ☺ = __ ☹ = __

The Teacher's Pocket Guide for Effective
Classroom Management, Second Edition, by Tim Knoster

BEHAVIOR PROGRESS REPORT (MIDDLE OR SECONDARY CLASSROOM)

Student name: _____

Teacher name: _____

2 = Excellent
1 = Satisfactory
0 = Unsatisfactory

Be responsible	Classroom entry/ start of class period	Class period until end of class period	Daily total
Keep my hands, feet, body, and objects to myself.	2 1 0	2 1 0	2 = _____ 1 = _____ 0 = _____
Say nice things to other people.	2 1 0	2 1 0	2 = _____ 1 = _____ 0 = _____
Follow adult directions the first time.	2 1 0	2 1 0	2 = _____ 1 = _____ 0 = _____
Date: _____		**Grand Total**	2 = _____ 1 = _____ 0 = _____

The Teacher's Pocket Guide for Effective
Classroom Management, Second Edition, by Tim Knoster
Copyright © 2014 Paul H. Brookes Publishing Co., Inc. All rights reserved.

MONITORING ACHIEVEMENT OF 4:1 RATIO

Date/time of probe: _____

Student names	Reinforcement received from teacher	Total	Redirection received from teacher	Total	Ratio of + to −
	+ + + + + + + + + + + + + + +		− − − − − − − − − −		
Whole class:					

BEHAVIOR CONTRACT

Student name: _Carl_   Today's date: _10/10/13_

Relevant staff name(s): _John Smith, Jane Goode, Carly Smith, Bob Pevey,_
Isham Kalou

Target behavior (behavioral expectation):

Be respectful: Use appropriate language. One person speaks at a time. Listen and follow directions the first time. Speak only at appropriate times; listen to others when they are speaking. Use an indoor voice when speaking.

Data collection procedure:

Use a good behavior chart with "+" for appropriate and "–" for inappropriate
behavior. Teachers and Carl independently evaluate Carl's behavior twice per
class period (halfway and at end of each class).

Reinforcement procedure (what and how often):

Carl can choose from a Choice Box (e.g., box containing homework pass,
10 minutes of extra computer time) at the end of each day when he has
earned 7 of 10 "+."

What must student do to earn reinforcement?

Be respectful: Use appropriate language. One person speaks at a time.
Listen and follow directions the first time. Speak only at appropriate times;
listen to others when they are speaking. Use an indoor voice when speaking.
7 of 10 "+" earned each day.

Consequences for failure to meet behavioral expectations:

Carl will not earn access to Choice Box. Other relevant consequences
deemed necessary by teacher(s).

Bonus for exceptional behavioral performance:

When Carl meets expectations 5 consecutive days in a row, he may make a
random choice from the Grand Prize Box (e.g., box containing coupons to
local sandwich shop, two free movie passes with free popcorn and large drink).
When Carl earns two consecutive bonus picks, we will renegotiate the contract.

Signatures of all relevant people: _____ _Carl_ _____
                                   _____ _John Smith_ _____
                                   _____ _Jane Goode_ _____
                                   _____ _Carly Smith_ _____
                                   _____ _Bob Pevey_ _____
                                   _____ _Isham Kalou_ _____

GUIDANCE FOR STARTING THE
CONVERSATION ABOUT SCHOOLWIDE
POSITIVE BEHAVIOR INTERVENTION AND SUPPORT

- In reality, it is unlikely that there will ever be a "convenient" time to try to initiate a conversation about SWPBIS in a traditional school setting. As such, your degree of success will have less to do with the fact that you have initiated the discussion and more to do with how you go about starting the discussion.

- Contextual factors will have a large impact on how you approach initiating the discussion. For example, you might approach starting the conversation with your building administrator in one way if he or she has been in the position for many years and has little knowledge of PBIS. However, you may approach getting the conversation started in an entirely different manner if your building administrator is relatively new and/or has (at least some) understanding of PBIS. You will want to carefully think through (analyze) such contextual factors in your planning. In general, it is often most helpful to frame the discussion around whole-school measures of achievement in broaching the topic with building administrators and embedding how your classroom fits in to that bigger picture.

- Along these same lines, starting the conversation with your fellow teachers requires some thoughtful planning. Try to identify one or two (or a few) teachers who you feel may be most open to having a conversation about prevention of behavioral problems and regaining instructional time. In general, it is often helpful to frame the discussion around how to recapture instructional time that is being increasingly lost due to behavioral matters in tandem with discussion about student achievement in talking with your teaching colleagues.

- You may find it helpful to network with teachers in current PBIS schools who themselves have some experience in initiating similar conversations in their respective schools before their schools adopted a PBIS approach. Conferences that focus on positive behavior support (e.g., APBS annual conference) and professional organization and/or project websites emphasizing schoolwide application of positive behavior support (e.g., http://www.pbis.org) can often times help you make such connections if you do not have such connections already in place.

TIPS FOR TEAMING WHEN DESIGNING AND IMPLEMENTING A STUDENT-CENTERED BEHAVIOR SUPPORT PLAN

- The process of designing and implementing student-centered positive behavior support plan (BSP) requires a team approach that begins with the student and his or her family and includes educators, other community resources, and support agencies involved with the student.

- As the complexity of the student needs increase, it becomes increasingly important that the team include both sources of natural support (e.g., people from the community) and formal services (staff from other child-serving systems). Teaming within the context of a wraparound process can help provide a holistic approach to service design and delivery, as well as to provide a viable way in which to coordinate services that prioritize meeting the needs of the student within the context of his or her family and community.

- Acknowledging both the fact that conflict (in the form of differences of opinion) is neither inherently constructive nor destructive and the volatile nature of designing and implementing a BSP, the team needs to clearly establish basic ground rules for operation that all team members agree to adhere to in order to constructively manage conflict within the team. The team is encouraged, at a minimum, to employ the following ground rules and processes in designing and delivering a BSP:

  - Agree on use of person- and family-centered processes.

  - Agree on language, avoid jargon, and hold one another accountable.

  - Use people's names in discussions.

  - Agree that only one person speaks at a time.

- Set clear goals and time frames in each meeting. Also consider assigning roles each meeting to help the team function (e.g., timekeeper).

- Facilitate everyone's involvement in meetings; avoid the situation of a few team members dominating the meeting.

- Wherever possible, include the student as a member of the team.

- Periodically discuss at the end of the meetings how the team is functioning.

- Avoid arguing blindly for positions, avoid statements of absolutes (e.g., "always," "never"), and remember that the focus is on socially valid outcomes.

- Practice what you preach; be supportive to all to express their thoughts by remembering the Golden Rule.

- Be honest.

- Strive to reach consensus as opposed to simple majority on important matters. All team members need to be able to support the plan in order to achieve sustainable results.

- Identify a plan facilitator (point person) whenever multiple sources of support will be used (e.g., various child serving systems, local community members, family members and friends).

- If or when things go wrong, avoid finger pointing and casting blame. Address the question "What would it take to make things work better?" when statements such as "This isn't working" arise.

- Focus on strengths and celebrate progress.

GUIDING THOUGHTS FOR ORGANIZING A STUDENT-CENTERED BEHAVIOR SUPPORT TEAM

- Designing a comprehensive BSP requires a collaborative team approach.

- Student-centered behavior support is a problem-solving process for addressing the support needs of the individual students as well as others involved with the student.

- Student-centered behavior support is assessment based. Interventions and supports are directly linked to environmental influences and hypotheses concerning the function of the student's problem behavior.

- Student-centered behavior support usually involves multiple interventions and supports that are provided in a coordinated manner.

- Student-centered behavior support is proactive, emphasizing prevention, by changing the environment and teaching alternative skills.

- Student-centered behavior support is designed for use in everyday settings using typically available resources (the support plan must fit the classroom/school setting).

- Student-centered behavior support holds a broad view of success that includes 1) increases in the acquisition and use of alternative skills, 2) decreases in the incidence of problem behavior, and 3) improvements in quality of life.

- Seek administrative support. Start by discussing the need to develop a student-centered BSP with the building administrator.

- An individualized BSP is likely needed in the following cases. In these cases, establish a team comprising all relevant people involved with the student (people who interact with student regularly and/or who will live with the results of the interventions and support).

- The student's challenging behavior persists despite consistently implemented classroom-based interventions.

- The student's behavior places the student or others at risk of 1) harm or injury and/or 2) exclusion and devaluations (e.g., in the form of multiple suspensions or expulsion).

- School personnel are considering more intrusive and restrictive procedures and/or a more restrictive placement for the student as a result of increasing degrees of problem behavior.

LINKING STRATEGIES AND INTERVENTIONS TO HYPOTHESES

A		–	B	–	C	
Slow triggers (setting events)	Fast triggers (antecedents)	–	Problem behavior	–	Actual consequence	Perceived function

Prevention Strategies

These strategies are identified to address the *A* part of the *A-B-C* Chain (also referred to as the fast and slow triggers or antecedents and setting events) that is/are associated with occurrence of problem behavior. Look at the triggers noted in the team's hypothesis statement, and identify things that can be changed instructionally to

- Remove or modify exposure of the student to those triggers

- Block or neutralize the adverse impact of those triggers if they can't be altered

- Add exposure to desired things (positive triggers) for the student

- Intersperse easy with more difficult tasks in the ebb and flow of instruction

Teaching Alternative Skills

These strategies focus on the *A*, *B*, and *C* parts of the *A-B-C* Chain. There are three types of alternative skills to emphasize:

- Replacement behavior: Look at the identified function (e.g., escape difficult writing tasks or gain teacher attention) in the team's hypothesis statement, and identify an alternative behavior that the student can be instructed to use that serves the same function as the problem behavior. Then instruct the student to use this replacement behavior to obtain the desired outcome (payoff). Remember, you are not reinforcing the problem behavior; you are simply providing an acceptable way in which the student can obtain the function (e.g., in the case of gaining teacher attention, teach the student to raise hand *and* provide timely attention when the student raises his or her hand).

- General skills: Look at the identified skill deficits in your team's hypothesis statement (which most likely would be noted as a slow trigger, e.g., poor reading skills), and identify general skills to instruct that will help address those skills deficits (e.g., provide instruction to improve reading comprehension skills).

- Coping skills: It is prudent to build in to a BSP the direct instruction of coping skills to enable the student of concern, when feeling frustrated or upset, to use to self-calm. Target simple, physical things that do not require a lot of external materials to facilitate generalization of use of the instructed coping skill(s) to any environment (e.g., deep breathing skills).

Consequence Strategies

- Reinforcement for appropriate behavior: Look specifically at the alternative skills your team has targeted, and look to provide sufficient levels of acknowledgment to the student as he or she acquires and uses these skills over time.

- Responding to problem behavior: Plan to specifically use redirection procedures (e.g., stop, redirect, acknowledge appropriate behavior as previously described in Chapter 8). Be sure to redirect the student, as needed, to use the targeted alternative skills. Then provide reinforcement for compliance in using the alternative skills. Remember, you are *not* reinforcing the student's problem behavior. Rather, you are reinforcing (even within the context of your redirection) the student's use of targeted alternative skills (remember to use behavior-specific praise along these same lines).

KEYS TO IMPLEMENTING A
STUDENT-CENTERED BEHAVIOR SUPPORT PLAN

- Remember, providing student-centered (individual intensive/tertiary level) behavior support typically requires a *team* approach.

- Be clear about the team's intended outcomes from the onset of design and implementation. In general, successful implementation of a BSP should result in 1) reductions in problem behavior, 2) increases in acquisition and use of socially acceptable alternative skills, and 3) meaningful outcomes from the student's and student's family's perspective.

- The behavior support team should meet on a scheduled basis to review performance data and determine needs for changes in the BSP. All plans, even when effective, will require varying forms of modifications over time.

- Keep in mind that in most cases a multicomponent approach is required, and as such, the BSP should reflect prevention strategies, teaching alternative skills and reinforcing both the acquisition and use of alternative skills in tandem with effective and efficient ways in which to redirect problem behavior.

- Be sure to address the needs of the members of the team implementing the BSP to best ensure consistent implementation.

- There is no set time frame within which to expect desired results from implementing a BSP. The behavior support team should identify what they view as a reasonable time frame to use as a guide as they monitor progress on a regular scheduled basis.

- If reasonable progress is not being realized, start by ensuring that the interventions and supports are being consistently implemented as designed. If the BSP is being consistently implemented, consider modifications to the existent interventions and supports (once again using the hypotheses that summarized the results of the FBA as your team's navigational device). Specifically focus on modifications in preventative, teaching, and consequence interventions and supports. If your team continues not to realize reasonable progress you may need to expand on the FBA and redevelop hypothesis statements concerning the nature of the student's problem behavior—and in turn develop a new BSP. Consider the integration of the process to design and implement a BSP within the context of a comprehensive wraparound approach with the student and his or her family in the event sufficient progress continues to be elusive.